The Book
for
YOUNG
MUSICIANS

This edition produced
in 1996 for
Shooting Star Press Inc
230 Fifth Avenue
Suite 1212
New York, NY 10001

© Aladdin Books Ltd 1996

Designed and produced by
Aladdin Books Ltd
28 Percy Street
London W1P 0LD

Printed in the Czech Republic
ISBN 1-57335-148-2

Some of the material in this
book was previously published
in the *Young Musician
Plays* series.

CONTENTS

**Written by Alison Hunka, Philippa
Bunting, Simon Walton, Paul Archibald,
and Alan Blackwood**

**Illustrated by Ron Hayward,
David West, and David Russell**

The Book
for
YOUNG
MUSICIANS

VIOLIN

The violin is probably the best known of all orchestral instruments. Some of the world's greatest music owes its beauty to the violin. Several other instruments are similar to the violin in construction and in method of playing. These include the viola and cello and they are all members of the violin family. This book explores how the violin works, the origins of the instrument, and how it has evolved to the present day. With the help of illustrations, the player is guided through first steps, to more advanced techniques.

FLUTE

The flute is a popular woodwind instrument which serves as the high "soprano" voice in orchestras, bands, and woodwind groups. Most flutes are now made of metal, but they are part of the oldest musical instrument group, the woodwind family. The most common other members are the recorder, oboe, piccolo, bassoon. *The Book for Young Musicians* includes an introduction to musical theory, as well as guidelines on how to play the flute.

UCTION

PIANO

The piano is a keyboard instrument which produces a greater range of musical sounds than most other instruments. On a piano, a musician can play melody and harmony at the same time. It is an instrument used in lots of different types of music, including jazz and rock. Most classical composers have written for the piano as a solo instrument and in combination with other instruments or with singing. *Young Musicians* shows how a piano works, its origins, and tips on playing.

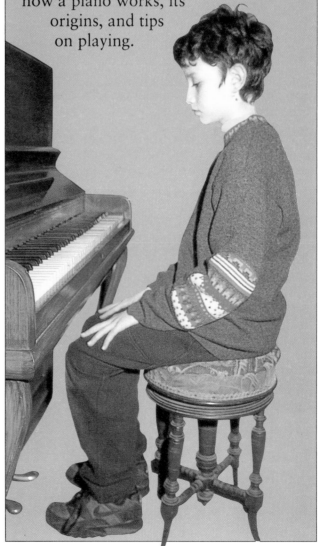

TRUMPET

The trumpet is an important orchestral wind instrument. It is used as a military instrument because of its brilliant and powerful tone. It is a member of the brass family together with the trombone, French horn, tuba, and other instruments. This book explores how a trumpet produces sound, the origins of the instrument, its use in jazz music, and in the modern orchestra. It also includes tips and exercises for solo and duet practice.

The Book
for
YOUNG
MUSICIANS

VIOLIN

AND STRINGED INSTRUMENTS

CONTENTS

INTRODUCTION

The violin is one of the best loved of all musical instruments. The beauty of its shape is matched by a beauty of tone. The violin is a member of the family of stringed instruments. It is capable of a wide range of musical expression: the sound of the violin can be almost as varied and as moving as the human voice.

When a violin string is plucked or bowed it starts to vibrate. These vibrations pass through the bridge to the soundpost inside the violin. The sound is then amplified throughout the hollow inner chamber, and escapes through the f-shaped sound holes in the belly.

SOUNDPOST
The soundpost helps to withstand the pressure of the strings on the bridge and the belly.

BELLY

CHIN REST

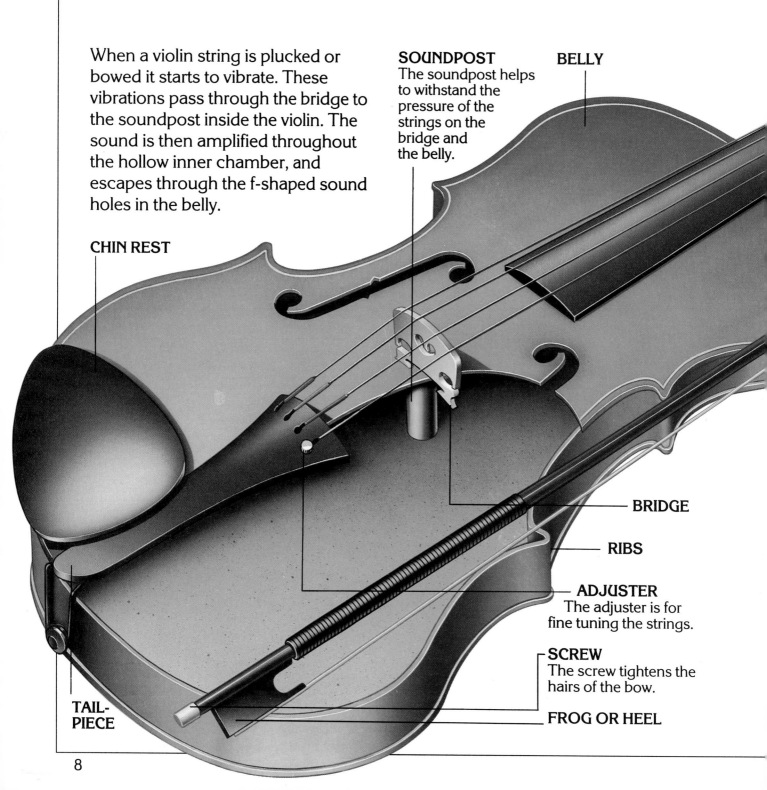

BRIDGE

RIBS

ADJUSTER
The adjuster is for fine tuning the strings.

SCREW
The screw tightens the hairs of the bow.

FROG OR HEEL

TAIL-PIECE

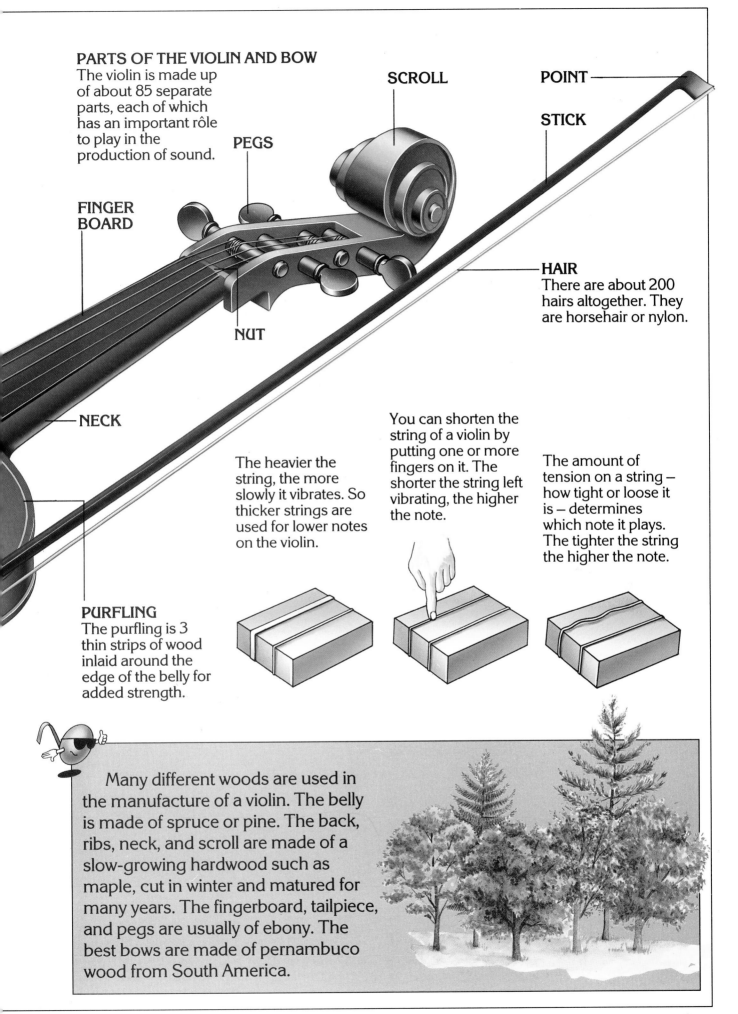

PARTS OF THE VIOLIN AND BOW

The violin is made up of about 85 separate parts, each of which has an important rôle to play in the production of sound.

SCROLL

POINT

STICK

PEGS

FINGER BOARD

NUT

HAIR
There are about 200 hairs altogether. They are horsehair or nylon.

NECK

The heavier the string, the more slowly it vibrates. So thicker strings are used for lower notes on the violin.

You can shorten the string of a violin by putting one or more fingers on it. The shorter the string left vibrating, the higher the note.

The amount of tension on a string – how tight or loose it is – determines which note it plays. The tighter the string the higher the note.

PURFLING
The purfling is 3 thin strips of wood inlaid around the edge of the belly for added strength.

Many different woods are used in the manufacture of a violin. The belly is made of spruce or pine. The back, ribs, neck, and scroll are made of a slow-growing hardwood such as maple, cut in winter and matured for many years. The fingerboard, tailpiece, and pegs are usually of ebony. The best bows are made of pernambuco wood from South America.

GETTING TO KNOW THE VIOLIN

Before you begin to play, you must find a way of holding your violin that feels comfortable and natural. Ideally your violin should feel part of you. You should be able to hold it just tightly enough to keep it from slipping, but not so tightly that your shoulder and neck muscles tense up. Being relaxed when you play will make everything much easier.

GETTING READY TO PLAY

Stand with your feet shoulder-width apart. Hold the back of the violin against your stomach, with your left hand around the neck and your right hand under the chin rest. Now stretch your arms out to the left, turn the violin and place it on your left shoulder. Let the instrument lie along your left collar-bone. Turn your head to look toward the scroll, and the side of your jaw will fall naturally onto the chin rest.

SITTING POSITION

When violinists have to play for long periods of time, for example in an orchestra, they usually play sitting down. This is less tiring on the legs, but makes it harder to maintain a comfortable violin position. Standing up allows the player greater freedom of movement, so violinists usually stand up when they practice or play solos. If you do have to play sitting down, both of your feet should be flat on the floor. Your knees should be apart and your back should be straight but not stiff. Hold your violin as you would if you were standing.

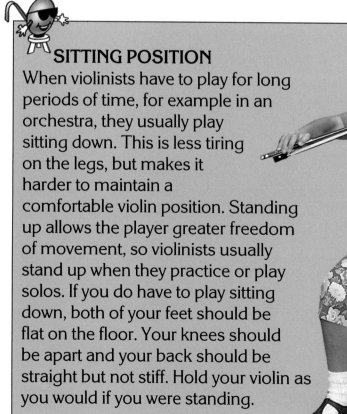

HOLDING YOUR VIOLIN

The violin can be held without any help from the left hand – try it and see! However, the left hand can provide some useful support. Bring your left thumb up to the place where the neck meets the body of the violin and let your fingers rest above the strings.

PLUCKING

You are now ready to try plucking. Gently tug at one of the strings with the first finger of your right hand, and let go. Pluck the string about 1in (2 cm) from the end of the fingerboard. Bring your hand around in a circle, and come back to pluck a different string.

FIRST POSITIONS

In its early days, the violin was held against the player's chest with the thumb under the frog of the bow. Later the violin was held loosely under the chin, without allowing the head to rest on the instrument (there were no chin rests in those days). The player's elbow was held against his or her side. Both positions are still used by some contemporary folk musicians. The position we use today allows us to play more difficult music. Early bows were shaped like an archer's bow, with the wood bent outward from the hair rather than toward it.

MAKING A START

On the previous page you got to know your violin a little, and heard some of the sounds it can make. Now you are ready to learn more about what those sounds are, and how they can be put together to make music. Each of the violin's four strings is tuned to a particular note. The strings are named after these notes.

THE OPEN STRINGS

Starting with the lowest in pitch, the four open strings are G, D, A, and E. Pluck them in turn and say their names. Now try and sing the same notes. Can you hear how different the sounds are? Each string has its own individual character, like a person, and violinists make use of this to bring out the character of the music.

G D A E

TUNING THE VIOLIN

Tuning is something you may need help with at first, as the strings need to be

You can also buy sets of pitch pipes, with a note for each string.

at exactly the right tension and pitch for you to be able to play the right notes. You can tune the strings to a piano or to a tuning fork, which is more reliable. To change the pitch of a string you use the tuning pegs, or adjusters if you have them.

PLUCKING PRACTICE

Here is a simple tune for you to pluck. It will help you to get to know the four open strings. Play the large letters as long notes and the small letters as short notes. Try this tune line by line. Listen to the notes as you play them. Then try playing the piece all the way through, with the long and short notes making the right rhythm.

A D A D   GGGG D D

A E AA E   EEEE A A

D AA DD D   G GG D D

A E A E   AAAA D D

WHAT DID YOU HAVE FOR BREAKFAST?

Now try inventing, or improvising, music for yourself. In the last piece, the long and short notes made up a rhythm. Make up your own rhythm now, by saying your name and address aloud. You could also try saying what you had for breakfast.

Now pluck along as you speak, to make a musical picture of the rhythm of the words. Choose different strings to suit the different things you are saying. You could even try having a conversation between two strings!

HOW STRINGS ARE MADE

All violin strings used to be made from sheepgut. Then it was discovered that winding aluminum or silver thread around the gut meant that strings could be made stronger and thinner. Now nylon or plastic is often used instead of gut for the central core, and the strings are wound with aluminum or copper wire. The material from which the string is made affects the quality of the sound it produces.

READING THE NOTES

In written music, notes are shown as dots on a set of five lines called a staff. The higher the notes appear on the staff, the higher they are in pitch. Being able to read musical notation means that you can play music written by other people.

NAMING THE NOTES

Musical notes are named after the letters of the alphabet, from A to G. After G the letters begin again. In the diagram on the right, the open strings of your violin are represented in musical notation, and as notes on the keyboard. Open string D is just below the five lines of the staff. The note above, on the lowest line of the staff, is E. The note in the space above is F, the note on the next line is G, and then comes open string A. All the open strings appear in spaces.

The treble clef symbol (below) indicates the pitch range of the notes for the violin.

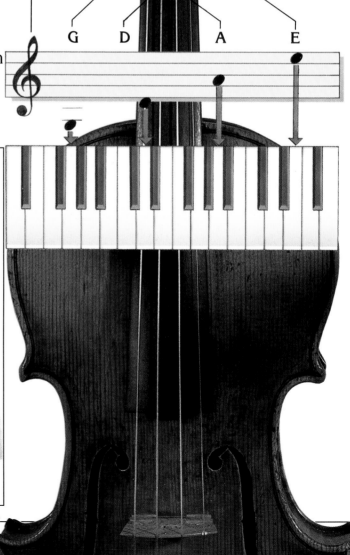

G   D   A   E

LEDGER LINES

The pitch of a note means how high or low the note is. Notes like open string G are pitched too high or low to fit on the staff. Little extra lines, like steps on a ladder, reach up or down to them. These are known as ledger lines.

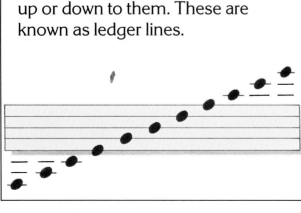

OPEN STRING PRACTICE

Now that you know what the open strings of your violin look like in notation, you are ready to practice reading them. All the notes below are the same length. You'll see that the written notes form a visual image of the notes you hear as you play. The higher the notes appear on the staff, the higher the sound you hear.

As you read the music, look ahead at the notes that come next. As you play one note you should know what the next one is, so that your hand leaves the string traveling in the right direction for the next note. The vertical lines below are bar lines. They organize the music into easy-to-read units called bars or measures.

THE FIRST VIOLINS

The violin-like instrument in this medieval French miniature is a *lyra de bracchia*, an ancestor of the violin. When the violin first appeared in the 16th century, it was mainly used as an instrument to play music at dances and weddings, and was not regarded very highly. More popular with composers and musicians was the family of viols. These stringed instruments were made in various sizes, and were designed to be played together in groups or consorts. They were held between the knees, and played with a bow. They had frets to guide the fingers of the left hand, as guitars do today. By the 18th century viols had been replaced by the violin and its family of instruments.

ADDING THE BEAT

The beat of a piece of music is like the ticking of a clock or the pulse of a metronome. Most of the time it stays regular, but the rhythm – the pattern of long and short notes – varies within this basic beat. On this page you can see how long and short notes look when they are written down.

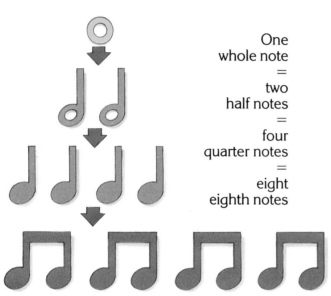

One
whole note
=
two
half notes
=
four
quarter notes
=
eight
eighth notes

Notes of different time values are written in different ways. Each of the rows shown above uses up the same amount of time in the music.

The whole note is the longest single note here. It takes up the same space in time as two half notes, four quarter notes, and eight eighth notes.

RESTS

In music, the silence between notes is just as important as the notes you play. In written music, silence is represented by symbols called rests. Different symbols represent silences of different time values, which correspond to the notes above. When you come to a rest in musical notation, try to think of it as a silent note, and remember to give it its full time value.

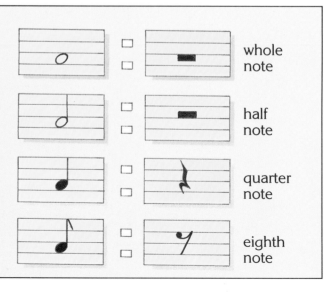

whole note

half note

quarter note

eighth note

Different pieces of music have different numbers of beats in a bar. The time signature at the beginning of the music tells you about this. The bottom number tells you what note forms the basic beat. In all the examples which appear above, it is a quarter note beat.

The top number tells you how many beats there are in a bar. The first example above, 2/4 time, has two quarter notes to the bar, or the equivalent made up of notes of other time values. 3/4 time has three, and 4/4 time four quarter notes to the bar. Try out these examples.

TRADITIONAL SKILLS

The violin plays a major part in the Eastern European musical tradition. Gypsy violinists (right) are famous for their skillful playing and the mournful quality of much of their music. The fiddle has also been the most popular folk instrument in North America for a long time; on the opposite page you can see two early American musicians. In the United States, the fiddle has a repertoire of over 1,000 tunes, and some fiddlers are said to know more than 400 from memory.

DOWN TO BUSINESS

You are now familiar with the open strings. On this page you can find out how to sound some of the notes in between. These notes are made by placing the fingers of your left hand on the strings in different positions.

For playing the violin the fingers of your left hand are numbered as shown.

3
2
1

Put your fingers on the strings as shown. Your thumb, helping to support the violin, touches the neck opposite your first and second fingers.

NUT

1

2

3

Putting your finger on the violin string shortens the length of the string that vibrates, and produces a higher note. The gap between the nut and the first finger is the same as the gap between fingers 1 and 2 (a whole step); the gap between fingers 2 and 3 is half that distance (a half step).

Pluck open string D with your left hand in place ready for the next note.

Put your left index finger down. Pluck the string to sound the note E.

Put your second finger down a little way from the first. This note is F sharp.

Add your third finger so that it touches your second. This note is G.

D STRING PRACTICE

This tune uses all the notes you have learned on the D string. Notice that the fingering has been marked over the notes to help you. Try plucking this exercise now. Then come back to it later and play it with the bow.

TRYING OUT THE A STRING

The finger pattern for the D string – a large gap between the nut and the first finger and between fingers 1 and 2, and half the distance between fingers 2 and 3 – works for the other strings too. Now try the pattern on the A string.

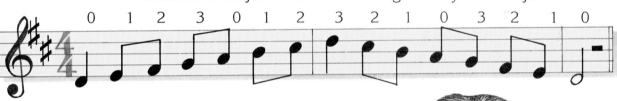

D MAJOR

Putting all these notes together, you can play your first scale, the scale of D major. The symbols in the "key signature" by the treble clef are sharps. Here sharps appear on the notes F and C, indicating the key of D major.

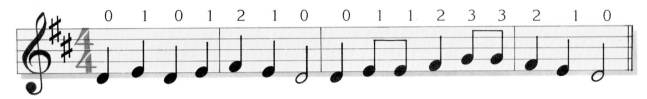

ANTONIO VIVALDI

Antonio Vivaldi (1678-1741) was one of the most important and prolific composers for the violin. He lived in Venice, and entered the priesthood at 15. He was nicknamed " the red priest" because of his red hair. Vivaldi wrote nearly 400 concertos for the violin. A concerto is a composition usually for a solo instrument and orchestra. Vivaldi's most famous work is "The Four Seasons," a set of four concertos, one for each season of the year.

TAKING UP THE BOW

A violin without a bow is only really half an instrument. The bow releases the violin's "voice." *Pizzicato* (plucking) is a useful effect in music, but the bow unlocks the violin's full range of expression. The first step is to become as comfortable with the bow as you are now with the violin itself.

HOLDING THE BOW

Practicing your bowhold with a pencil first is a good idea. Make a circle with your right thumb and two middle fingers. Your thumb should be opposite your fingers, so that you can feel your thumbnail. Now take up your bow in the same way, holding it at the frog end. Your thumb should rest under the stick of the bow opposite your middle fingers. Your index finger now joins the middle two over the stick, with space between each finger. The tip of your little finger balances on top of the stick.

Place your bow on a string, with the frog end about ½ inch from the bridge.

Draw the bow slowly down toward the point and back again. As your bow hand gets further away from the violin, guide your bow so that it remains parallel to the bridge. Try bowing each string in turn without touching any of the other strings.

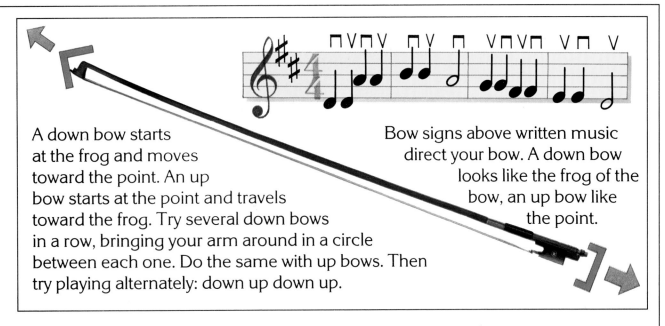

A down bow starts at the frog and moves toward the point. An up bow starts at the point and travels toward the frog. Try several down bows in a row, bringing your arm around in a circle between each one. Do the same with up bows. Then try playing alternately: down up down up.

Bow signs above written music direct your bow. A down bow looks like the frog of the bow, an up bow like the point.

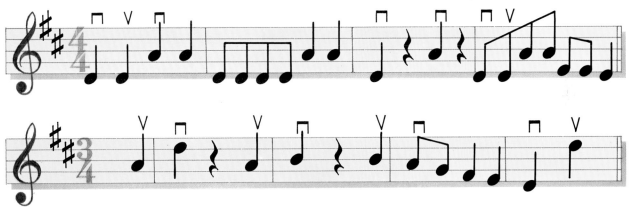

A down bow is often used on heavier beats, such as the first beat of the bar. An up bow is used on lighter beats.

Use the rests in the first piece above to make a circle with the bow, so that you are ready for the next down bow.

CARING FOR VIOLIN AND BOW

Like any musical instrument, your violin and bow need to be well cared for. Don't put your violin next to a radiator, or leave it outside overnight; if it gets too hot or cold the wood may crack. Rosin your bow regularly, but never touch the hairs of the bow with your fingers. When you finish playing, loosen your bow and wipe your violin with a soft cloth to remove old rosin. Stock your violin case with spare strings and rosin. Last but not least – keep your fingernails short!

SMOOTHING OUT THE NOTES

You can change the sound the violin makes by varying the way you draw the bow across the strings. Experiment with the speed of bow, and with the amount of weight you put on the string. Bowing close to the bridge produces a different sound. Now you are ready to try playing more than one note in each bow. This technique is called a slur.

WHAT IS A SLUR?

Singers often have one word to sing on each note. When they have one word to sing over many notes, they spread the word over all the notes in a slur. A violinist uses his or her bow to create a similar effect. You can also use slurs to vary the way you play a musical sentence, or phrase.

ONE BOW FOR MANY NOTES

So far you have learned to play with one bow to each note, so that the note and the direction of the bow change at the same time. In a slur, the bow continues to travel in the same direction as the note changes. In one bow you can sound a number of different notes.

PRACTICING SLURS

To play slurs you need to be able to do two things at once. Although they are performing separate activities, the movements of your two hands need to be coordinated, so that they work in time with each other. This is an important skill in violin playing. Practice it by putting one finger down on the A string. Start a down bow. Halfway through the bow, take your finger off. The bow should carry on smoothly, and should not jerk when the note changes. Do the same on an up bow. The noise you produce may sound like an ambulance siren!

Slurs can be between notes on the same string, or on different strings. In the second of these exercises, use your right elbow, not just your hand, to lead you from one string to the other. Then try the piece below.

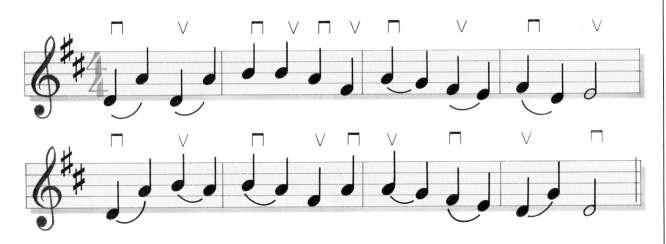

ANTONIO STRADIVARI

Antonio Stradivari (1644–1737) is generally acknowledged to be the greatest violin maker of all time. He worked in the Italian town of Cremona, and made over 1,000 instruments during the course of his career. Of these about 600 survive now, some of which are in museums. Many of Stradivari's instruments have been given individual names – two of his finest violins are called the "Alard" and the "Messiah."

MOVING ON

This page shows you how to play the other notes you can make using the simple finger pattern you learned on pages 18-19. With these notes you will be able to play two more scales: A major and G major. Once you feel sure of these notes, try picking out some simple tunes from memory – or make some up yourself!

SCALE OF A MAJOR

The scale of A major uses the same finger pattern as the scale of D major, but it is played on the A and E strings. Scales are patterns of large and small gaps (whole steps and half steps).

These gaps, or intervals, stay the same whatever note you start on. To preserve the pattern, the scale of A major has three sharps: F, C, and G. You can see them in the key signature.

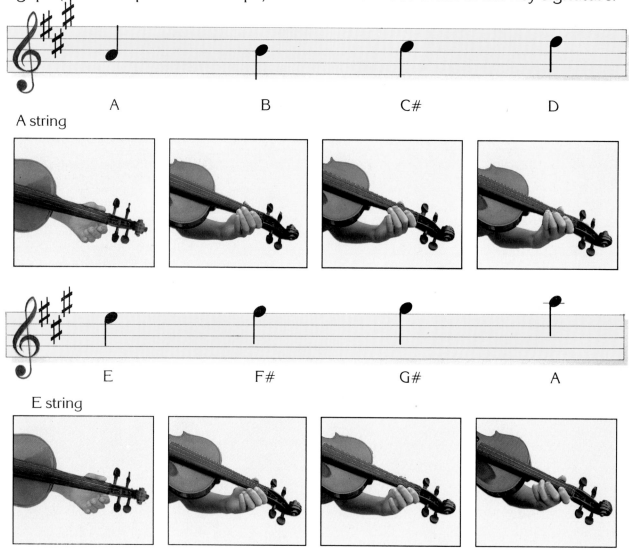

SCALE OF G MAJOR

The scale of G major uses the same finger pattern as the other two scales you have learned, but it is played on the G and D strings. G major has one sharp, F, in the key signature. Use one long bow to each note.

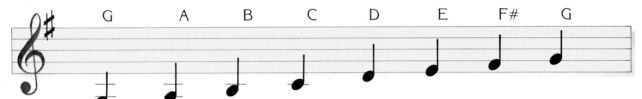

G   A   B   C   D   E   F#   G

GOOD AND BAD HABITS

Bad habits are easy to pick up and very hard to unlearn later. This is particularly true of playing the violin, because there are so many things going on at once that it is hard to keep track of them all! Some of the basic rules are as follows:

Don't do anything that makes you tense, or anything that hurts.
Keep your shoulders down and keep them loose.
Don't tighten the muscles in your neck when you get to a part of the music that you find difficult.
Stay as relaxed as possible. You'll find that you play much better, and are able to enjoy it more!

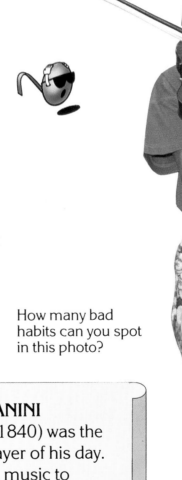

How many bad habits can you spot in this photo?

NICCOLÒ PAGANINI

Paganini (1782–1840) was the greatest violin player of his day. He wrote his own music to display his expertise. His musical genius and eccentric appearance led to rumors that he had made a pact with the devil to enhance his playing. His "Napoleon" sonata is played on the G string alone.

FIRST MELODIES

By now you may be starting to pick out some of the tunes you know from memory. This page gives you an opportunity to practice playing written music. Using everything you have learned, try out these melodies; as you play, remember to listen carefully to check that you are playing in tune, and producing a good sound.

THE LONESOME FIDDLER

Before you begin to play, study the music. Look at the key signature and the time signature. "The Lonesome Fiddler" is in 4/4 time, with four quarter notes to the bar.

Try clapping the rhythm of the piece before you start. As you play, think about the intervals between the notes, not just where you are going to put each finger. This will help you to play in tune. Don't start moving the bow until your fingers are in the right place – as you get more experienced at playing you will get quicker at doing this. Finally, enjoy playing the music – that's what it's all about!

RAINBOW WALTZ

"The Rainbow Waltz," like all waltzes, is in 3/4 time, with three quarter notes to the bar. Each piece of music has its own character, which you must try to bring out.

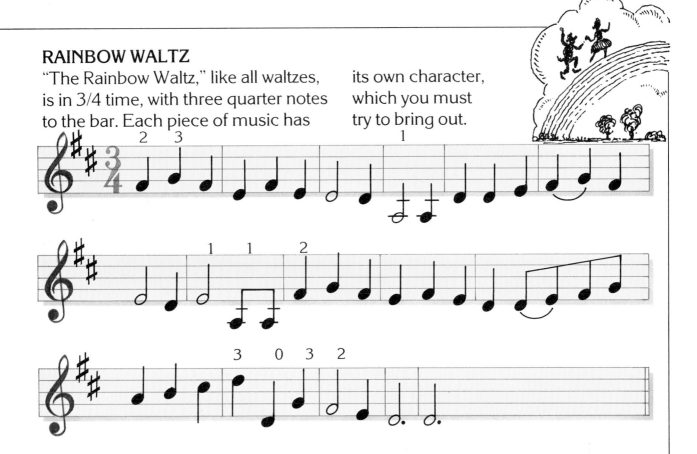

PLAYING WITH OTHERS

Many people learn to play the violin in a group. This is one of the best ways to learn, because you hear other people play and get used to playing with them. There are many methods for learning in groups. If you have the chance, join a string group or an orchestra. You may make new friends!

PLAYING TOGETHER

Playing with other people is one of the most exciting and rewarding aspects of learning an instrument. Playing with just one other person is a good place to start. A piece of music for two people to play is called a duet. One written especially for you appears below. It is written in the key of D major, with F sharp and C sharp in the key signature.

MUSIC BOX

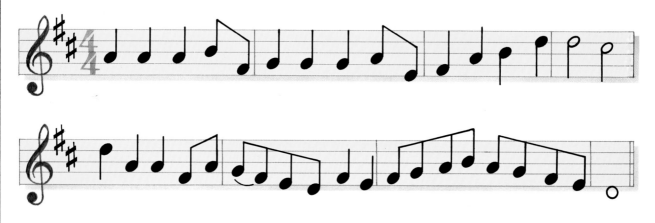

FIRST VIOLIN

In order to play successfully with someone else, you need to know your own part well. Start by trying the first violin part, which carries the melody. Then see if you can also play the second violin part, which is the accompaniment. Both parts are equally important! Finally, try playing this duet with a friend or with your teacher. When you put the two parts together, make sure both players start and finish at exactly the same time!

THE RANGE OF THE VIOLIN
The full range of the violin extends over four octaves (the scales you have learned so far were one octave scales). Some very difficult music uses the full range of the instrument, from one end of the fingerboard to the other. With work, there is no reason why you should not be able to play music like this in time, although pieces that are hard to play are not always the most rewarding musically!

SECOND VIOLIN
The second violin part is more complicated than the first, as it moves faster and crosses strings more often. When you play it with a partner, listen to make sure that the rhythm of your accompaniment fits with the tune. Give the rests their full value and listen to what the first violin is playing.

MUSIC BOX

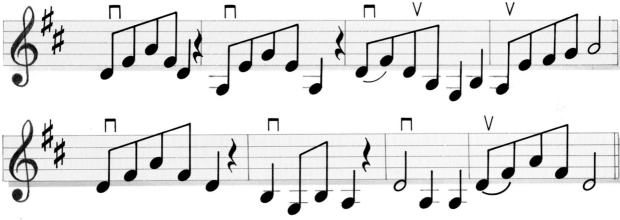

JAZZ VIOLIN
The violin can be used to great effect in jazz. This music is not written down, but is improvised (made up) by the players as they go along. Two of the most famous jazz violinists were Stephane Grapelli and Joe Venuti, both of whom often played in duos with guitarists. Nigel Kennedy is a classically trained violinist who also plays jazz.

THE WORLD OF THE VIOLIN

The variety of musical effects possible on the violin makes it one of the most popular of all musical instruments. All over the world, you will find people playing violins or similar kinds of musical instruments. The versatility of the violin makes it suitable for playing many different styles of music.

THE ORCHESTRA

There are more violins in the orchestra than any other instrument. They are divided into first and second violin sections. The first violins often play the melody, and the second violins play something different, which forms part of the accompaniment. Two players share each music stand, and all the players in a section play the same music. Violinists in an orchestra blend in their individual sound with the other violins in their section. In this way, a violin section sounds like one instrument.

THE CONCERTMASTER

The leader of a section sits at the front. All the other players follow what he or she does. The leader of the first violins is also concertmaster of the orchestra. This tradition dates back to the time when orchestras were smaller and didn't have conductors. The concertmaster directed the orchestra and played at the same time.

STREET MUSIC

The violin is light and portable. As a solo instrument, the music it produces is expressive and appealing. These qualities make it a good instrument for street music. You may have seen violinists playing in subway stations or in the open air, collecting money in a hat or in a violin case.

VIOLIN AND PIANO

When a violinist plays in a duo with one other musician, it is most often with a pianist. There is a huge repertoire of music written for this combination of instruments. In the majority of this music both instruments are equally important, in some earlier music the piano accompanies the violin.

STRING QUARTET

A quartet is a group of four musicians. A string quartet has two violins in it, which play different parts. The other instruments are viola and cello. As in an orchestra, the first violin is the leader of the group. Many composers wrote some of their most wonderful music for string quartet.

STRING FAMILY

The violin is the smallest member of the string family, and the highest in pitch. It was also the first to be invented. The violin's immediate relatives – the viola, cello, and double bass – can also be either bowed or plucked. As the body of the instrument gets bigger, so its range of notes becomes lower.

VIOLA, CELLO, AND DOUBLE BASS

The viola (below) is slightly bigger than the violin, and is held in the same way. The cello (right) is even bigger, and is played sitting down. The instrument is held between the player's knees, and rests on an endpin or spike. Largest and deepest is the double bass (far right), which has the same strings as the violin, but in the reverse order. Bass players play sitting on a high stool, or standing up.

THE CONCERT HARP

The other member of the string family with a regular place in the symphony orchestra is the concert harp. Each string of the harp produces one note when plucked; each of these notes can be lowered or raised half a tone by means of pedals. The characteristic sound of the harp makes it instantly recognizable, even when the whole orchestra is playing. Also related are the guitar and the zither, which is a folk instrument.

THE STRINGS IN THE ORCHESTRA

The stringed instruments form the mainstay of the modern Western symphony or chamber orchestra. Together the strings cover a range of over seven octaves. It is even possible to have an orchestra made up solely of string players – a string orchestra. The variety of effects possible with stringed instruments, such as *pizzicato* (see page 20) makes them very popular with composers.

ALTO AND BASS CLEFS

The lower stringed instruments read music written in different clefs, although both the viola and the cello sometimes use the treble clef. The viola usually plays music written in the alto clef (below left) and the cello uses the bass clef (right). So does the double bass, but its notes sound an octave lower than written.

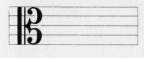 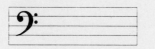

GEOGRAPHY OF THE ORCHESTRA

The diagram below shows how a symphony orchestra is usually laid out. The stringed instruments are spread across the front of the platform in a semicircle, ranging from the violins on the left to the double basses on the far right. The conductor stands at the front, surrounded by string players. If the piece is a concerto, the soloist stands or sits next to the conductor.

POSITIONS OF THE STRINGS

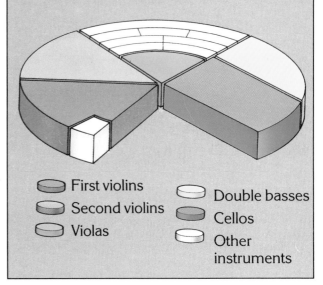

First violins

Second violins

Violas

Double basses

Cellos

Other instruments

The Book
for
YOUNG
MUSICIANS

FLUTE
RECORDER AND OTHER
WOODWIND INSTRUMENTS

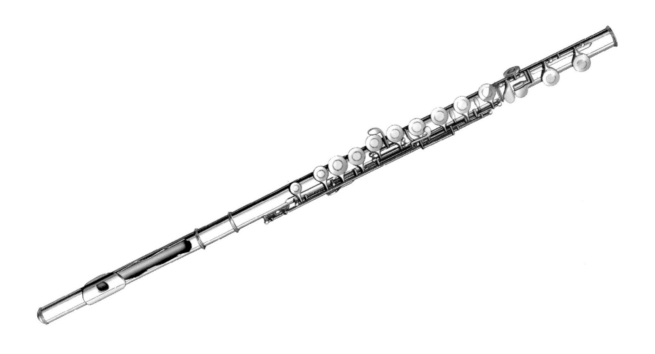

CONTENTS

INTRODUCTION

The flute family is of the world's oldest groups of instruments. It includes the modern side-blown, or transverse flute, recorders, fifes, and whistles. All of these are woodwind instruments, like the clarinet, oboe, and bassoon. In ancient times, flutes were used in sacred ceremonies to evoke spirits, and were sacred to the Hindu God Krishna.

The beautiful, pure sound of the flute is heard above the other instruments of the orchestra. The flute is a hollow tube, stopped at one end. Near the stopped end is a mouthpiece. The musician blows across the mouthpiece to cause the air inside the instrument to vibrate and produce sound. Other holes are bored along the body, to produce a range of notes.

Padded keys are suspended over the holes, on rods that are soldered on to the tube. Each metal key has a soft pad inside it. When you press down the key with your finger, the pad forms an airtight seal over the hole beneath, to alter the pitch of the note by lengthening or shortening it. A spring returns the key to its original position once you release it.

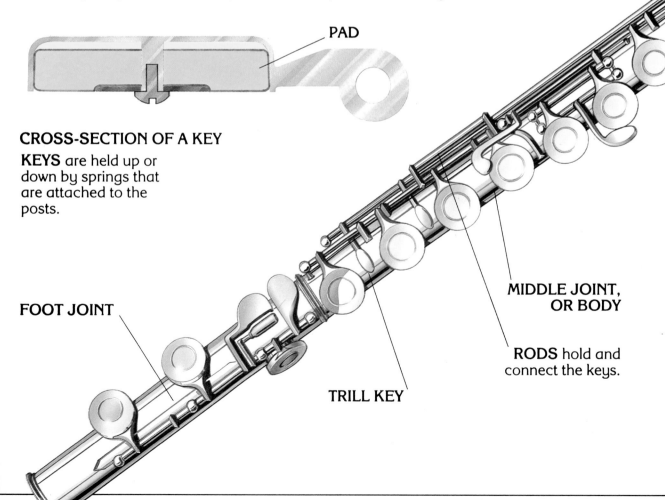

PAD

CROSS-SECTION OF A KEY

KEYS are held up or down by springs that are attached to the posts.

FOOT JOINT

TRILL KEY

MIDDLE JOINT, OR BODY

RODS hold and connect the keys.

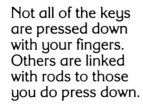

Not all of the keys are pressed down with your fingers. Others are linked with rods to those you do press down.

EMBOUCHURE, OR BLOW HOLE

LIP PLATE

RIB

SPRING

POST

HEAD JOINT

CROWN

CORK

The end of the flute is plugged with a cork squeezed between two metal disks. These are held on a threaded post which moves up and down the tube as you twist the crown.

Flutes and recorders are called woodwind instruments because they were originally made of wood. Today most flutes are made of metal, although wood is still used for the recorder and the piccolo.

In the 19th century, some show flutes were made of glass. Ivory, porcelain, and carbon fiber have also been used. Cork, felt, cardboard, and even the lining from cows' abdomens are used in the manufacture of the pads.

Professional flutes are often made of solid silver. Student flutes are often made with a nickel-silver alloy, which actually contains no silver but is a kind of white brass, plated with silver. Flutes can also be made of gold.

GETTING TO KNOW YOUR FLUTE

Your flute is made in three parts. Take care when putting it together, as it is quite easy to damage. Hold the parts of the flute where there are no keys, and go slowly and carefully at first.

Ease the middle and foot joints together first, twisting them back and forth. Line up the rod on the foot with the keys on the body.

Twist and slide the head into the body next. Line up the middle of the blow hole with the centers of most of the keys.

Now take up your flute and position your fingers above the keys as shown below and on page 41. Your left thumb is held against its key at an angle. Your flute is supported at the base of the first finger of your left hand, and by your right hand thumb, which goes behind, not underneath, the flute. These two contact points, with your chin, keep the flute supported and balanced. Your other fingers are free to work the keys.

It is important to be relaxed and comfortable when playing the flute. Get ready to play by holding your flute pointing out in front of you, with the head joint above your left shoulder. Swivel the flute around to the right, until your shoulders are stretched. Turn your head to the left and bring your flute up to your mouth. You should be looking over your elbow, as shown above.

Stand up straight with your feet shoulder-width apart. Don't lock your knees.

CARING FOR YOUR FLUTE
Protect your flute from sudden changes in temperature. Never leave it near a radiator; metal may warp, and wooden piccolos can crack. Warm up your flute simply by playing or by holding it in your hands. Blowing harshly through the flute may warm it too quickly. Clean your flute after you have finished playing. Moisture will rot the pads, and can swell and crack wooden instruments. Thread a cotton cloth through your cleaning stick. Clean each joint separately. Push the stick into the head gently. *Don't allow the stick to scratch the inside.* Dust the outside with a clean paintbrush. Don't adjust keys, springs, or screws unless you are quite sure of what you are doing. Ask your teacher to help instead.

MAKING A START

Your first sounds on the flute are made by blowing into the head only. Place the lip plate under your bottom lip, so you feel the edge of the hole against the edge of your lip. Make an "oo" shape with your mouth, and blow across the hole as if you are blowing a bubble.

Cover the open end of the head joint with the palm of your hand at first. Keep the sides of your mouth relaxed and your breath even.

Now take your hand off the end. Practice long notes, keeping the sound steady. It may take a while to produce a good sound.

The shape that you make with your lips is called an embouchure (pronounced om-boo-sure). Use a mirror to check that yours is in the center of your mouth. Direct your breath toward the opposite rim of the blow hole.

When you blow across the hole, some air passes into the flute, and some passes over it. This causes the air inside the flute to vibrate. Try rolling the flute in and out to cover less and more of the hole.

Study how the flute keys in the photo relate to the circles and shapes in the diagram. Only the keys you touch are shown. Later in the book keys colored red should be pressed down. White keys should be left up.

Check that your fingers are positioned over the keys as shown here. Make sure that you are placing the pads of your fingers in the center of the keys. Your right hand thumb should not poke out from under the flute.

The fingering for notes on the flute will be shown throughout the book in diagrams like the one at top right.

EARLY FLUTES

The flute family is very ancient. The earliest flutes that have survived are thought to be 20,000 years old. They were sometimes used in religious rites. Early flutes were made of many different natural materials, such as bone, stone, wood, horn, and shell. Historians believe that flutes originated in central Asia. They were carried by traders along silk trading routes, to reach China around 5000 B.C. The Chinese flute, the *Tse*, has remained virtually unchanged since then. The flute reached India and Mediterranean lands as late as 200 B.C. Flutes have been played by shepherds tending their flocks for thousands of years. Different kinds of flutes are found in many parts of the world, including Tibet, below.

FIRST NOTES

Written music can look difficult, but it's really very simple. Musical notes are named after the letters of the alphabet, from A to G. After G the letters begin again. Notes appear on a set of five lines, called a staff. The position of notes on the staff tells you how high or low they sound.

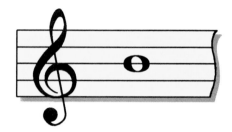
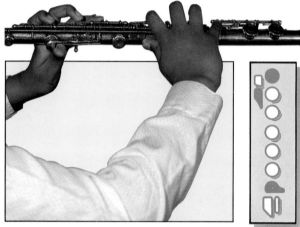

Note B appears on the middle line of the staff. Press down the single thumb key and first finger of the left hand, and the right hand little finger.

Note A is a tone below B, and is written in the space below the line for B. Press down the single thumb key.

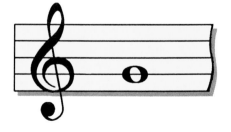
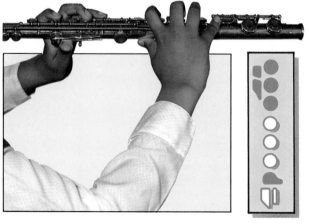

The note G is a tone below A and sits on the line below it. Notice that the notes become lower the more keys you press down.

Now try the tunes below, using B, A, and G. The next page deals with notes of different lengths. Make all the notes the same length here, and play them steadily and evenly. As you play, remember to stand straight, with relaxed shoulders and knees. Keep your head up. Music can be used to create all kinds of moods. The mood may be indicated at the beginning of the music, as it is in the third piece below.

The treble clef at the start of the music indicates the pitch of notes. Breathe deeply and blow the air out steadily as you play.

Listen to your sound. Are you making the best tone you can? Practice these pieces until you can play them through confidently.

Slow and sad

BAROQUE FLUTES

One of the first European side-blown flutes was the *Schwegal*, played by German soldiers in the 12th century. By the Baroque period (from around 1600 to 1750), flutes were cone-shaped, wider at the head end, and tapered at the foot. Johann Joachim Quantz (1697–1773), right, was an important flute player and teacher. He was court composer to Frederick the Great of Prussia, and taught Frederick the flute.

ADDING THE BEAT

The beat, or pulse, is vital to a piece of music. It is what gets your foot tapping or your fingers drumming to the tune. In written music, long and short notes are represented by different symbols. The beat remains constant, at whatever speed you have decided to play. The rhythm, or pattern of long and short notes, varies within the basic beat.

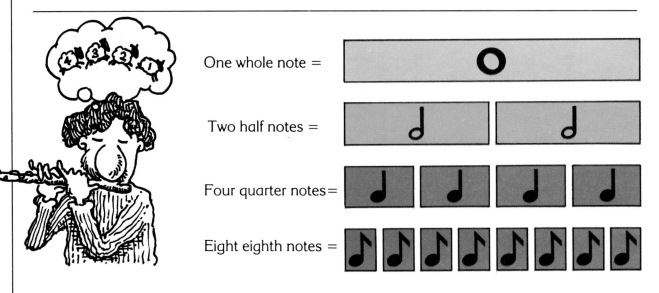

One whole note =

Two half notes =

Four quarter notes =

Eight eighth notes =

Symbols for the notes of different time values are shown above. Reading from the top down, each note is twice the time value of the one below it.

Memorize the symbols, then try counting or clapping each line. Most pieces are counted in quarter notes, so count four for a whole note and two for a half note.

RESTS

Silence can be as important as sound in music. In written music, silence is shown by symbols called rests. A rest often makes the audience more alert, waiting to hear what is coming next. Rests of different time values correspond to all the notes you have met. Think of rests as silent notes, and count them just as carefully as played notes.

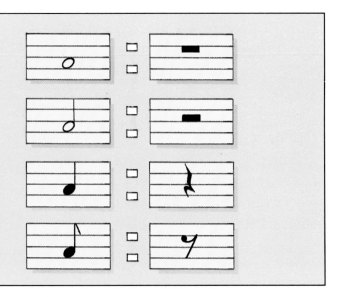

Written music is divided into bars, or measures. Pieces of music have different numbers of beats in the bar, shown by the time signature after the treble clef. The bottom figure tells you what note indicates the beat, and the top figure tells you how many there are in a bar. So 3/4 time has three quarter notes in a bar, and so on. Try clapping or counting the pieces before you play them. A dot after a note increases its time value by half.

At walking speed

Briskly as if running

Dancing

CHARLES NICHOLSON

Baroque flutes had six or seven holes. In the 18th century, holes were added to produce clearer notes. Keys were introduced to cover the holes that the flutist's fingers could not reach easily. Flutes were still conical.

Charles Nicholson (1795–1837), right, was an English flute player renowned for his full sound and brilliant technique. He lived in London, where flutes became very popular in the 19th century. Flute clubs appeared all over the city, and learning the instrument was seen as part of the schooling of an English gentleman.

MOVING ON

Over the next two pages there are six new notes, which will help you play more tunes. Changing notes between C and D will really test how well you have your flute in balance, as every finger has to change except for the little finger of the left hand. Make sure your flute does not roll back as you play.

C can be difficult to balance, as you have only your left hand first finger and right hand little finger down. Keep your right thumb against the flute, and make sure it doesn't roll back.

If you have difficulty playing the low notes, make sure that you are keeping your head up. It is tempting to move your head up and down as you try to play high and low.

E is your lowest note yet. You may have to press the keys more firmly for the low notes, as old flute pads may leak. Try not to make this a habit. It will shorten the life of the pads.

Practice the new notes on their own first, then try the exercise below. Look at the time signatures and clap

the rhythms before you play. The signs linking the notes in the first piece are slurs.

SHARPS AND FLATS

Sharps and flats, the black notes on a piano, fit between the "natural" notes, the white notes on a piano. B flat is a half step, or half a tone lower than B — try them both and listen to the difference. F sharp is a half step higher than F. Fingerings for these notes are given here. The piece below includes them.

TONGUING

So far you have blown evenly to produce a continuous tone. The technique of tonguing breaks up the stream of sound, to begin notes more cleanly. Tonguing makes little sound, but makes the start of the note cleaner.

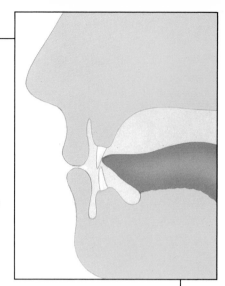

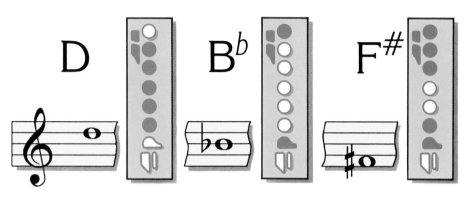

Tongue by saying "te" as you blow a note, quickly touching your teeth with your tongue, as shown above. When reading music, tongue each note, unless notes are joined with a slur, as shown below.

DESIGNER OF THE MODERN FLUTE

Theobold Boehm (1794-1881) was a German flutist and goldsmith. He was responsible for the creation of the modern flute. Inspired by the sound of Charles Nicholson, Boehm decided to make a flute that would produce loud, clear notes. He designed an instrument with all the holes needed to produce the notes in the octave. He invented the system of keys still used today, with a few minor changes. Boehm's early models were still cone-shaped, but later versions had a cylindrical body and conical head.

THE SECOND OCTAVE

You can play a sequence of seven natural notes, going up from E to D. After D the sequence begins again with E. This is an octave. The higher E is played with the same fingering as the E you know. Make your embouchure smaller, and speed up your air stream. Move your jaw forward slightly and direct your airstream a little higher.

All the notes from E to C in the second octave are produced in the same way. Practice them, using the fingerings you know. The first picture shows the shape of the air column inside your flute for the notes in the first octave. The air vibrates twice as fast when you play notes in the

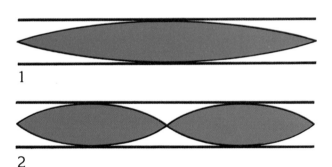

1

2

second octave. The other diagrams show how the air column vibrates as even higher notes are played. Learn to recognize the sound of an octave by practicing the first piece below. High notes appear above the staff. You will notice that extra lines, called ledger lines, reach up to the notes.

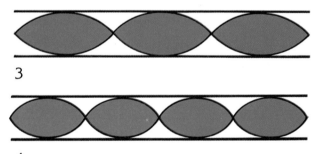

3

4

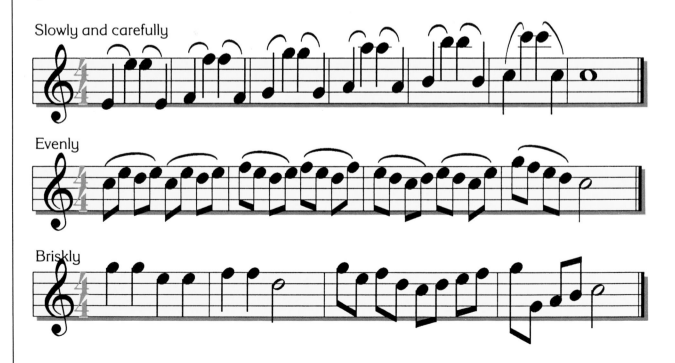

Slowly and carefully

Evenly

Briskly

GOOD AND BAD HABITS

Bad habits are easy to develop, and hard to stop once they become familiar! Bad posture can cause a lot of pain when you are older. Remember to stand up straight and keep your breathing deep and even. This will allow you to play more notes without gasping for breath, or feeling faint from lack of oxygen!

Listen to yourself as you are playing, and try to improve your tone. Practice regularly, every day if possible. Try to practice at the same time each day, or you may never get around to it!

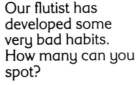

Our flutist has developed some very bad habits. How many can you spot?

🍬 BUYING YOUR OWN FLUTE

If you decide to buy your own flute, ask your teacher for advice. If possible, go to a speciality flute store, where you will find a good choice of instruments. The store should check each flute thoroughly before putting it out for sale.

Take a piece of music you know to the store so that you can try out various flutes. Try a few of the same model if you can, as they can vary. If possible, arrange to take the flute home with you for a trial period, so you and your teacher can test it.

Hold your head and your flute up, but keep your shoulders down and relaxed. Don't cross your legs when you play! Keep your feet shoulder-width apart. When reading music, stand at a sensible distance from the music stand, otherwise you may start lowering your head to read.

FIRST MELODIES

Now you are ready to try some melodies. Below are well-known pieces by Mozart and Verdi. Practicing a tune you know will leave you free to concentrate on your sound. You may also be able to listen to the same melodies performed by famous musicians.

PRACTICE AND PERFORMANCE

Use a mirror when you are practicing, to check your posture, hands, and embouchure. In an examination or concert, try to relax, and remember to breathe deeply. Make yourself comfortable: adjust your music stand to suit your height, and make sure you can see both your pianist and audience.

THEME FROM CLARINET QUINTET   MOZART ARR. WALTON

Study the music carefully. This piece is in 4/4 time, with four quarter notes to the bar. Clap the rhythm. A dot above or under a note indicates that it should be played *staccato*, as a short note. Don't rush staccato notes, and don't end a note with your tongue. Dotted notes are worth one and a half times their usual value. The notes with double tails are sixteenth notes, worth half the time value of an eighth note. The dotted eighth and sixteenth together make up one quarter note beat.

A metronome (left) will help you keep to the beat when you are practicing. If you find you can't keep up, set the metronome on a slower speed.

LA DONNA È MOBILE

VERDI ARR. WALTON

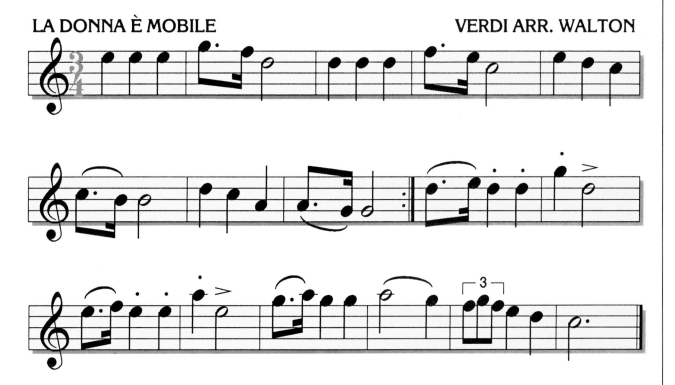

The double bar line with two dots in the middle line is a repeat sign. Return to the start and play the music again, before going on. The symbols like hairpins are accents. Blow these notes more strongly. Near the end is a triplet of three eighths, played in the time usually taken for two.

MARCEL MOYSE

Marcel Moyse (1889–1984), right, was a brilliant flutist and great character. He influenced the French flute school, which became famous for warm and expressive playing. In the 1930s Moyse had a demanding schedule as a concert artist and teacher. He often traveled overnight between Paris, Geneva, and other European cities on his beloved motorcycle. Geoffrey Gilbert (1914–1989) introduced the French style of playing to Britain. Gilbert was an important 20th century British flutist.

REACHING THE THIRD OCTAVE

The sound you make on the flute depends on your control over the air you blow out. Practice regulating your breathing. Lie on the floor with your hands on your stomach, just under your rib cage. Breathe in and out slowly and deeply. As you expand your rib cage, air is drawn into your lungs. Your hands should rise with your stomach.

THE THIRD OCTAVE

The fingerings in the third octave are more complicated. To sound the notes, you need to tighten your embouchure and speed up your air jet, as you did for the second octave. Notes may sound squeaky at first, but will improve with practice.

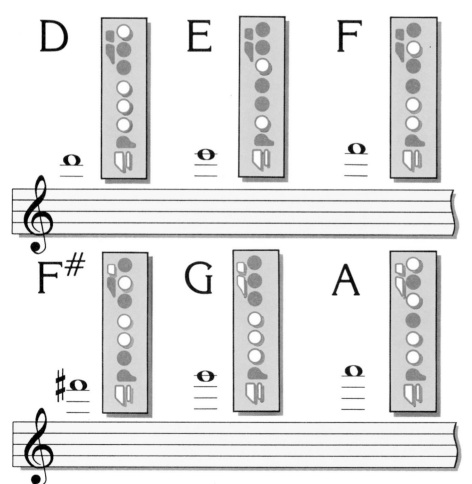

Practice the changes of fingering between these notes. Don't practice the flute only in the third octave; your lower octaves will suffer and so will your neighbors!

Now practice the notes D to A in all three octaves, playing loudly and softly. Memorize these new fingerings and try to hit each note cleanly as you move up the octaves.

The exercise below will help you to practice finger changes. It is in 4/4 time. As you change notes, move all your fingers together, quickly and smoothly. Slur the notes as written, and listen for slips as you change fingering. Pay attention to the natural signs in bars eight and nine. They tell you to play F natural, not F sharp.

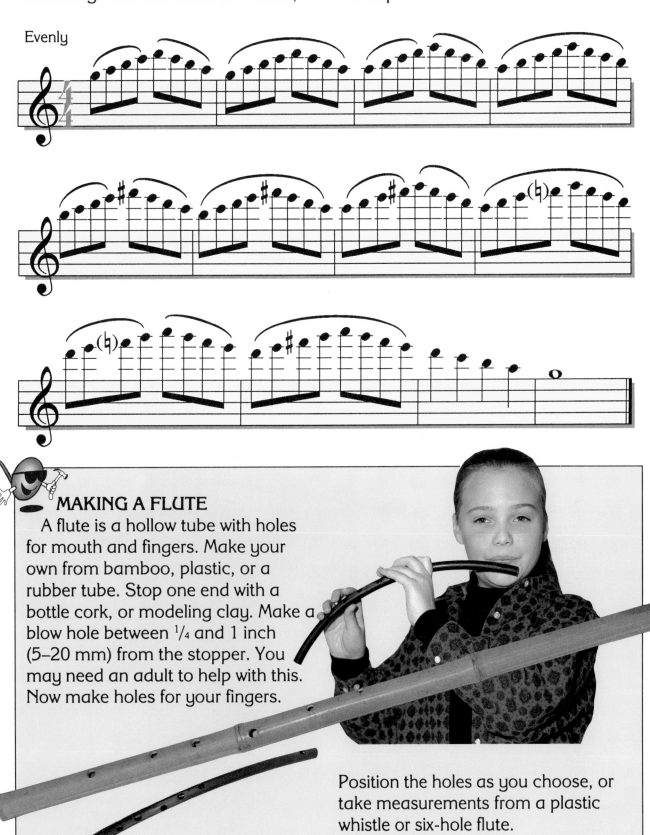

Evenly

MAKING A FLUTE

A flute is a hollow tube with holes for mouth and fingers. Make your own from bamboo, plastic, or a rubber tube. Stop one end with a bottle cork, or modeling clay. Make a blow hole between ¼ and 1 inch (5–20 mm) from the stopper. You may need an adult to help with this. Now make holes for your fingers.

Position the holes as you choose, or take measurements from a plastic whistle or six-hole flute.

PLAYING TOGETHER

Playing with others can be fun. Below are two pieces for you to play with friends or with your teacher. Neither has the parts written out one below the other, as you would expect. The first is a canon. One player begins, and the second starts when the first reaches the note marked 2*. Other players can begin as the first reaches 3*, 4*, and so on.

CANON　　　　　　　　　　　　　　　　　　　**TALLIS ARR. WALTON**

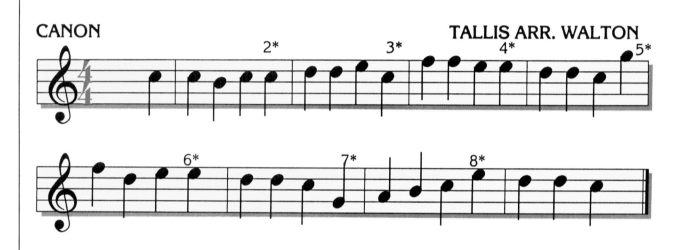

Good posture will help your sound. When you are sight-reading, try not to lean forward toward the music. Your head will come down and disturb your embouchure. When sharing a music stand, arrange your flutes so that you and your partner don't bump into each other. It may be easier if the player on the left puts his or her flute behind the other player. Don't swing around with your flute up! This piece is in 4/4 time and begins on the fourth beat of the bar. Count yourself in aloud, and try to keep to an even tempo (speed) throughout.

A duet is a piece of music for two players. This one is special, and should be placed flat between two players. Both start at the same time and read the music from opposite sides. Again, count yourselves in and keep an even beat. Try to reach the end at the same time!

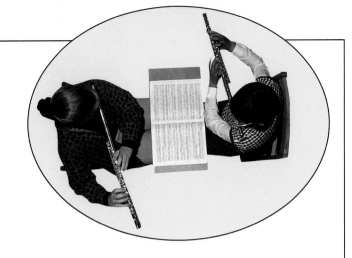

UPSIDE-DOWN MINUET

DOPPLER EFFECT

During the 18th and 19th centuries, *virtuoso*, or very skilled performers, would tour the cities of Europe giving concerts. The Doppler brothers, Karl and Franz, were a famous duo of flutists who toured in the middle of the 19th century. To prevent the possibility of tangling flutes, and so that audiences could see the flying fingers of both players, Karl Doppler had a special flute built that he could play to the left.

FLUTE FINGERING CHART

Below is a fingering chart complete up to top F#. Where two fingerings are given for one note, the alternative will sometimes produce a better sound. Try them all.

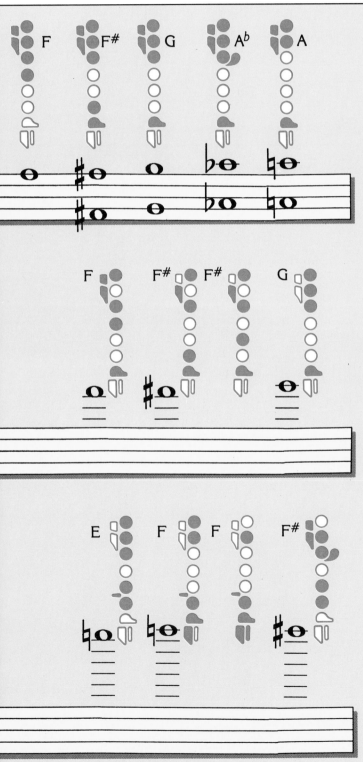

SPECIAL EFFECTS

Professional flutists use a variety of techniques to widen the range of notes they can produce.

VIBRATO

Vibrato is a technique which imitates the voices of opera singers. Try it once you can produce an even, pure sound. Without tonguing, make accented notes to a steady tone, as if you were saying "Ha-Ha-Ha ." Speed them up gradually, to form a vibrato.

fast passages, professional flutists use double or triple tonguing. Try it out for yourself. Practice saying "Te-ke " for double and "Te-te-ke" for triple tonguing.

MULTI-PHONICS

Multiphonics involves playing more than one note at once on the flute. Instead of moving cleanly up to the next octave, widen your airstream to cover both notes until they sound together. Other modern techniques include note-bending and key-tapping. For note-bending, move your jaw in or out to cover more or less of the hole with your top lip. This makes the note bend higher or lower. Key-tapping involves fingering loudly while not always blowing, so that the noise of the keys can be heard.

FLUTTER TONGUING

Flutter tonguing is popular in modern music. It is done by rolling a long "rrrrr " with your tongue, or by gargling in the back of the throat while blowing!

DOUBLE AND TRIPLE TONGUING

When tonguing very

PLAYING THE RECORDER

The recorder is a member of the flute family. At various times in history it has been more popular than the flute. Recorders are made of wood or plastic, and can be quite cheap to buy. The simplicity of the recorder makes it a good instrument for beginners, who may later change to the flute or another member of the woodwind family.

Blowing into a slot in the mouthpiece directs a stream of air against the edge of an opening called the fipple. Air flows alternately over and into the recorder, vibrating the air inside the instrument.

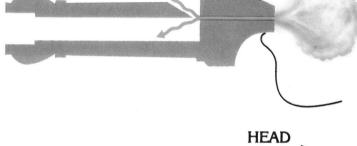

Notice how the fingerholes on the recorder correspond to the diagram below. The extra key in the diagram top right is for the left hand thumb, which fits underneath the recorder.

HEAD

MOUTHPIECE

FIPPLE

BODY

FINGERHOLES

FOOT

MICHALA PETRI

Michala Petri is one of the most famous recorder players today. She was born in Denmark, and made her first professional appearance at the age of eight. Michala Petri plays music from both the baroque and contemporary periods. She gives concerts all over the world, helping to restore the popularity of the recorder.

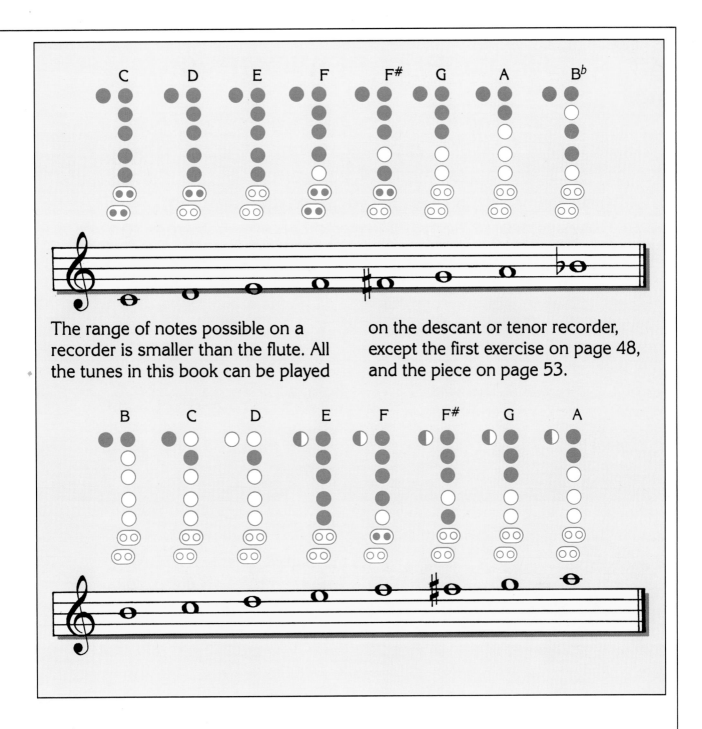

The range of notes possible on a recorder is smaller than the flute. All the tunes in this book can be played on the descant or tenor recorder, except the first exercise on page 48, and the piece on page 53.

The recorder was a popular instrument in the late Middle Ages, and has remained virtually unchanged since then. Much music from the baroque period now played on the flute was written for the recorder. Recently, recorders have become more popular again. There has been a great interest in hearing music from previous centuries played on the instruments for which it was written.

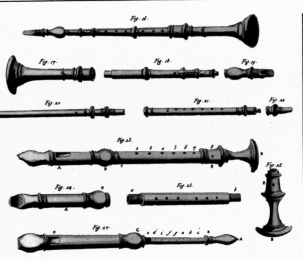

THE WORLD OF WOODWIND

The woodwind family includes the clarinet, oboe, English horn, bassoon, and saxophone, which use a single or double reed to make the air vibrate inside the instrument. Many different kinds of musicians play woodwind instruments, from the musician on the street corner to the folk or jazz player, and the professional in the concert hall.

Woodwind instruments are important in the orchestra, and are also used in chamber music, played by a small group of musicians. The wind quintet is a popular combination for chamber music, but almost any group of instruments can play. The position of woodwind in the orchestra is shown below right.

Flutes and other woodwind instruments are used as solo concert instruments or are accompanied by the piano, harp, or guitar. Baroque music now performed by the flute and piano was probably written for another keyboard instrument, the harpsichord. A good performer will communicate with both the accompanist and the audience.

If you get the chance, join a chamber group or an orchestra. Look for these orchestral pieces with famous woodwind passages:
Debussy, *L'après-midi d'un faune*
Stravinsky, *Petrouchka* and *Firebird*
Saint-Saëns, *Carnival of the Animals*
Prokofiev, *Peter and the Wolf*
Rossini, *William Tell Overture*

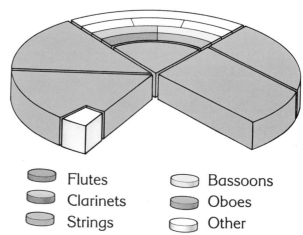

Flutes   Bassoons
Clarinets   Oboes
Strings   Other

JAMES GALWAY

James Galway is one of the best known flutists performing today. He is famous for his golden flute and the recordings he has made of concertos by Khachaturian and Rodrigo — the second of these was actually written for Galway. These pieces show off his bright, brilliant sound, and his superb tongue and finger technique.

Flute   Oboe   French Horn   Clarinet   Bassoon

The standard woodwind instruments are the flute, clarinet, oboe, and bassoon. Each instrument has larger or smaller relatives which produce a lower or higher sound. The little cousin of the flute is the piccolo, which is pitched an octave higher.

The clarinet, oboe, and bassoon all have vibrating reeds. The oboe has a double reed and a conical shape, opening out at the bottom. It produces a mellow sound. Richard Strauss and Vaughan Williams have written concertos for the oboe.

The clarinet has a single reed which vibrates against the mouthpiece. It has a beautiful, flowing sound and a range of three and a half octaves. Clarinets emerged in the 18th century, and were improved by Boehm. The bass clarinet is pitched an octave lower.

The bassoon has a distinct tone, which can sound comic or sorrowful. It, too, has a double reed. Its relative, the contrabassoon, plays an octave lower. The wind quintet (above) is completed by the horn, a member of the family of brass instruments.

TRUMPET
AND BRASS

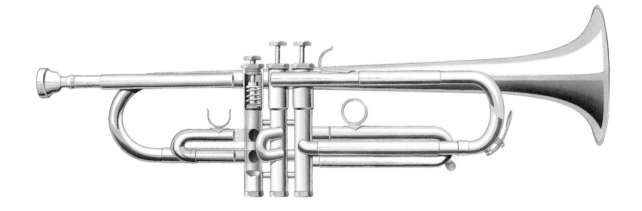

CONTENTS

INTRODUCTION

Welcome to the exciting world of the trumpet! As you will discover when you start playing, the trumpet has a unique sound, brilliant and beautiful. It can play very high and very low notes. These things take many hours of practice to master, but when you have worked through this book you will have a solid foundation on which to build.

The trumpet is a member of the brass family, like the trombone, tuba, and French horn. It is basically a length of hollow metal tube, opening out into a bell at one end, and with a mouthpiece at the other. When air passes through the tube, it vibrates and sound is produced.

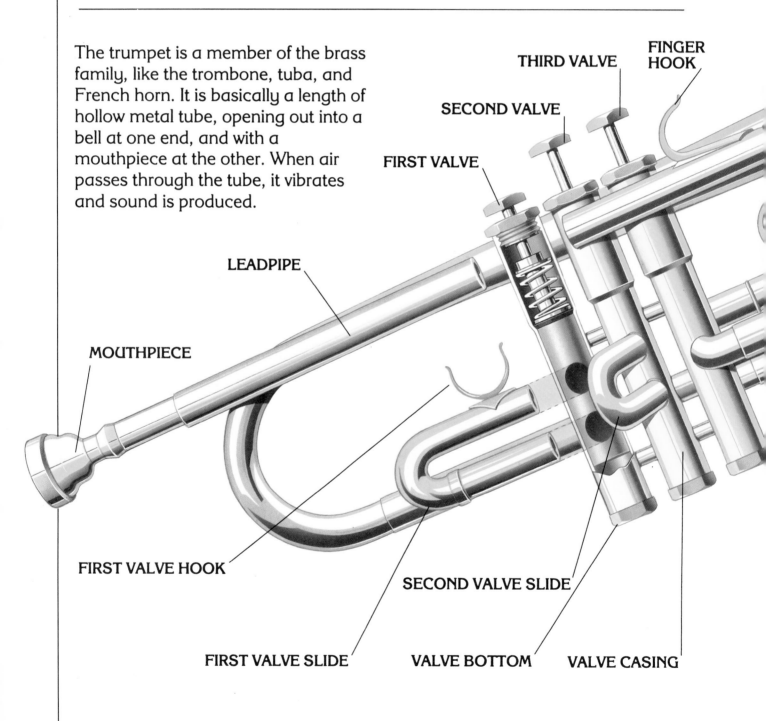

THIRD VALVE

FINGER HOOK

SECOND VALVE

FIRST VALVE

LEADPIPE

MOUTHPIECE

FIRST VALVE HOOK

SECOND VALVE SLIDE

FIRST VALVE SLIDE

VALVE BOTTOM

VALVE CASING

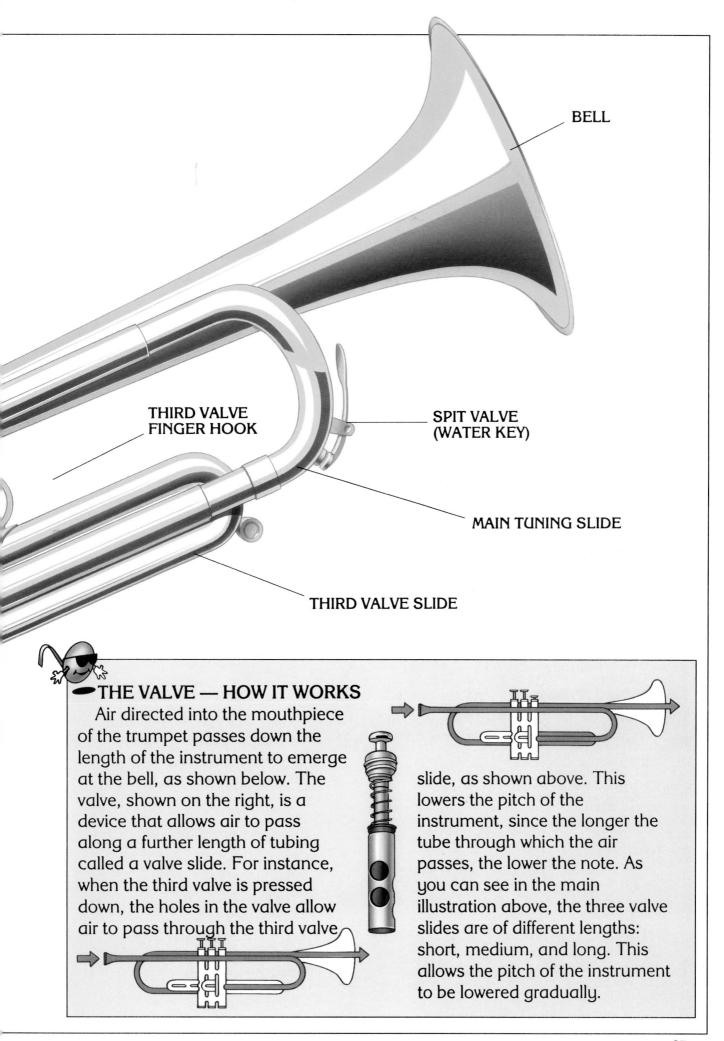

BELL

THIRD VALVE
FINGER HOOK

SPIT VALVE
(WATER KEY)

MAIN TUNING SLIDE

THIRD VALVE SLIDE

◗THE VALVE — HOW IT WORKS

Air directed into the mouthpiece of the trumpet passes down the length of the instrument to emerge at the bell, as shown below. The valve, shown on the right, is a device that allows air to pass along a further length of tubing called a valve slide. For instance, when the third valve is pressed down, the holes in the valve allow air to pass through the third valve slide, as shown above. This lowers the pitch of the instrument, since the longer the tube through which the air passes, the lower the note. As you can see in the main illustration above, the three valve slides are of different lengths: short, medium, and long. This allows the pitch of the instrument to be lowered gradually.

GETTING STARTED

Your trumpet should come supplied with a separate mouthpiece. It should be enclosed in a sturdy case, as it is very easy to damage metal instruments. A mute will affect the sound produced by your trumpet.

HOLDING THE TRUMPET — THE LEFT HAND

The trumpet should be held with your left hand around the valve casing. Your left thumb should be placed on the first valve casing, with your fourth finger through the finger hook (if there is one). The weight of the instrument should be on your forefinger, under the bell.

THE RIGHT HAND

Put the little finger of your right hand in the finger hook, as shown in the photograph below. Place the middle three fingers on the valves and place your thumb on the valve casing. Your right hand should not carry the weight of the instrument, and should remain as relaxed as possible.

SITTING POSITION

Find a chair that allows you to put both feet on the floor. Sit in the middle of the chair, with your body as straight as possible. Try not to slouch against the back of the chair. Keep as relaxed as you can, and try to prevent the bell from drooping!

STANDING POSITION

Make sure both feet are flat on the floor and a few inches apart. Keep your whole body, including your head, as straight as possible. Think of the trumpet's leadpipe as an extension of your nose, and try to keep the bell up!

TIP:
If you find the trumpet heavy and your shoulders start to ache, put the instrument down, and lift your shoulders up and down as fast as possible. They will feel a lot better afterward.

CARING FOR YOUR TRUMPET

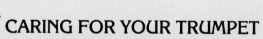

Taking good care of your trumpet is important. When you finish playing, remove the mouthpiece and put the instrument back in the case. Oil the valves every few days with trumpet valve oil. Make sure that all the slides can move. Apply trumpet slide grease or cream if necessary. If your instructor agrees, rinse the instrument out with dishwashing liquid and hot water every two weeks. If you take the valves off, lay them out in order, so they don't get mixed up. Dry it with a soft cloth.

EMBOUCHURE

The shape that you make with your lips when playing the trumpet is called an embouchure (pronounced om-boo-sure). It is the basis of all your playing, so it is important to get it right from the beginning. With your lips in the correct position, you will produce sound through the trumpet, not by blowing, but by "buzzing."

THE "BUZZ"

If you take two blades of grass, place them alongside your two thumbs and blow between them, you should be able to make a loud squeaking sound. This happens because the two blades of grass are vibrating together very quickly. When playing the trumpet the principle is similar, but we don't use grass — we use our lips!

Look at the photograph, make the same shape with your lips, and try to produce a buzzing sound, like a bee. It might take a little while to get the hang of it, but keep trying. Push the corners of your mouth down as shown here.

When you are confident with buzzing, place the mouthpiece on your lips as shown below. Place it in the middle of your mouth, with half on your upper lip and half on your lower lip. As you put the mouthpiece to your lips don't change from the "buzz" position.

Don't put the mouthpiece toward either side of your mouth, as shown below, only in the middle. Don't put the mouthpiece too low on your top lip — make sure you have half the mouthpiece on top, half on the bottom. Never blow your cheeks out!

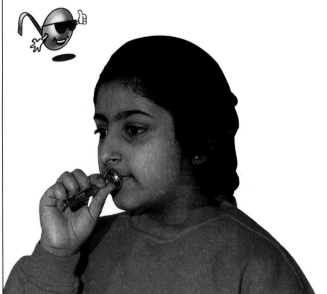

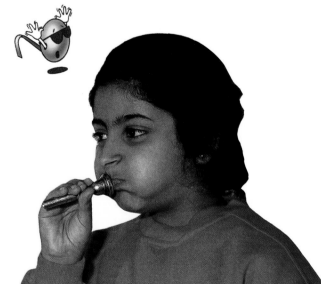

68

FIRST NOTES

At last we are ready to go! Place the mouthpiece back on the trumpet. Start "buzzing," then place the mouthpiece in the center of your embouchure and your first note should be heard. It will probably be a low note. Don't worry if it doesn't work right away, you will soon get used to the feel of your lips vibrating.

Middle C is called an open note because none of the valves are pressed down. In music it looks like this.

Press the first and third valves and buzz for the note D. D is above C and appears in the space above it.

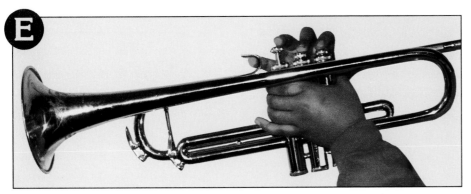

Press the first and second valves to sound the note E. It sounds above D and appears on the line above it.

EARLY NATURAL TRUMPETS

Trumpets and horns date back before Roman times. They were used by soldiers in battle, for ceremonies, and for hunting. Early "natural" trumpets had no valves (right), and could only play a limited range of notes. Bach and Handel wrote very high music for the natural trumpet.

READING MUSIC

Written music can look complicated, but it's really very easy. Notes are represented by black and white dots arranged on five lines called a staff. The staff is divided into units of time called bars, or measures, and the treble clef at the beginning indicates the pitch of the staff. The position of the notes on the staff tells us how high or low they are.

WRITTEN MUSIC

Musical notes are named after the letters of the alphabet, from A to G. After G the letters begin again. Reading from the bottom upward, the names of the notes on the lines in the treble clef are E G B D F (try remembering — Every Good Boy Deserves Fun). The notes on the spaces between the lines of the treble clef spell F A C E. The treble clef is the curly symbol that appears at the beginning of the music.

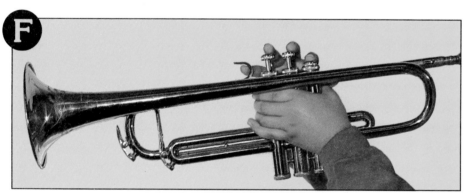

F

Here are two new notes to learn. The note F sounds above E. Buzz and press down the first valve.

G

G is an open note like C, with no valves down. G is higher than C — make sure you can hear the difference.

Now try all five notes:

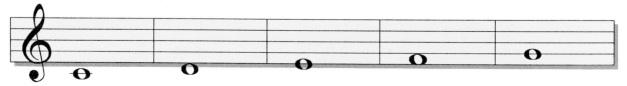

Once you feel confident playing five notes, try the next exercise, which adds on three more notes — A, B, and high C. The new fingerings appear beneath the notes. This is called a scale. It consists of seven notes followed by the original note one octave (or eight notes) higher. Play up the scale and then try coming down. Then try it from memory .

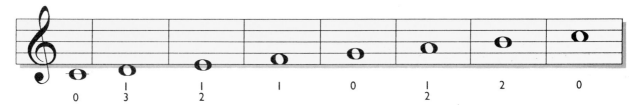

Don't worry if you find it difficult to play all the notes. Just play the ones you find easy — the rest will come, the more familiar you are with the instrument. If you can play all the notes, try the exercise below. Try to name all the notes that appear in this piece.

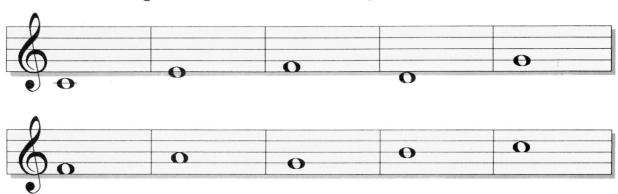

FRANZ JOSEF HADYN

Franz Josef Haydn was born in 1732, in the Austrian Empire. His talent for music was soon obvious, and he was admitted as a boy chorister at St. Stephen's Cathedral in Vienna. In 1761 he was employed by a wealthy nobleman, Prince Esterházy, near Vienna. This post allowed him to compose many symphonies, string quartets, and a few instrumental concertos. A concerto is a piece usually for a solo instrument accompanied by the orchestra. Haydn's last concerto was written in 1796 for the trumpet. It's one of the finest works written for the instrument.

ADDING THE BEAT

If you listen to your watch or clock, you will notice that it has a very regular "tick," or beat. The same applies to most of the music we play, but although the beat remains the same, the rhythm or pattern of notes constantly changes.

LONG AND SHORT NOTES

Longer and shorter notes are represented by different symbols in written music. The longest note shown here is the whole note, and the shortest is the eighth note. In terms of time, each of the notes shown here is worth two of the ones directly below it. Try counting or clapping each line: count four for a whole note and two for a half note. The exercises below use

One whole note =

Two half notes =

Four quarter notes =

Eight eighth notes =

the notes you have learned, with some of the new rhythms, or note lengths. Count or clap them through before trying them on your trumpet.

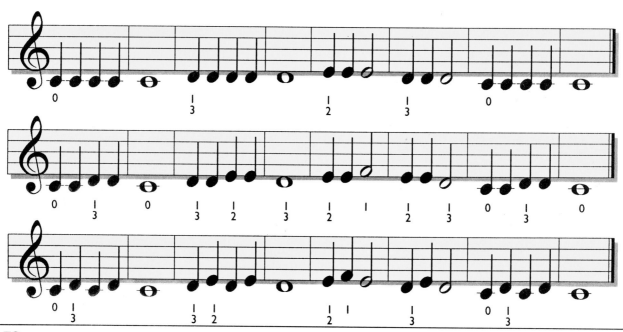

RESTS

As you have probably discovered, all this playing is quite exhausting! However, help is at hand, as music often has silences, called rests, built in. Different rest symbols correspond to all the note values you have met, as shown on the right. Rests can be very useful when we have to breathe. Try the exercises below, which include some of these new symbols.

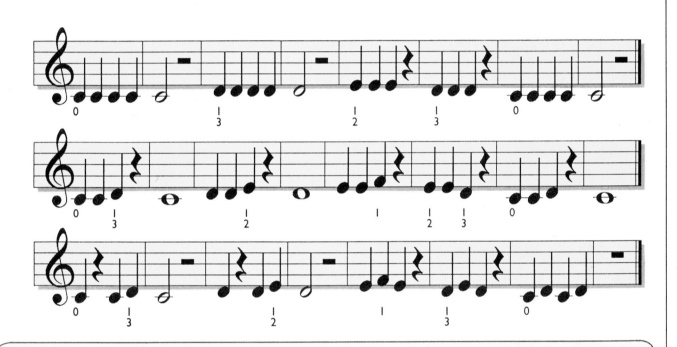

CLASSICAL TRUMPET

The trumpet as we know it today started to take shape with the invention of the valve in the early part of the 19th century. This meant that the trumpet could play more notes, and not be restricted to just a few. Composers such as Berlioz, Wagner, Ravel, and Mahler began to write more complicated music for the instrument. As the music developed, so the trumpet family grew, and instruments of different lengths, sizes, and even different numbers of valves were invented.

TONGUING

The tongue plays a very important role in trumpet playing. Not only does it provide the start of each note for us, but it also regulates the pitch of the note. It decides whether the note will be high or low. When playing the trumpet, your tongue moves up inside your mouth naturally as you sound higher notes.

NOTE PRODUCTION
The two most common ways to produce a note are: positioning the tip of the tongue behind the upper teeth to say "ta," shown right, or putting the tip of the tongue behind the bottom teeth and using the middle of the tongue to say "da." Move the tongue quickly to give a clear, crisp "attack."

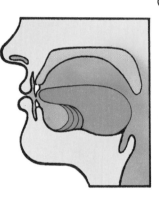

PITCH AND TONGUING
The position of your tongue affects the pitch of the note. When you say "Ah" loudly your tongue will be positioned low in your mouth (left). This is where your tongue will be when playing middle C. If you say "Eee" loudly, your tongue moves higher in your mouth (right). This is its position for high C.

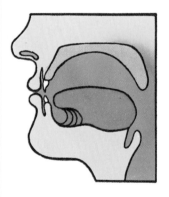

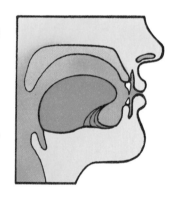

TIME SIGNATURES
At the beginning of each piece of music you will see two numbers, one on top of the other. This is called a time signature: the top number tells you how many beats there are in each bar.

The bottom number tells you what kind of note gets a beat. Three of the most common time signatures appear above. 2/4 time has two quarter notes to a bar, or the equivalent in notes of

other time values. 3/4 time, with three quarter notes, is used in waltzes and other music. 4/4 time, with four quarter notes to a bar, is also known as common time.

RHYTHM PRACTICE

These exercises use different time signatures. As you play them, imagine the ticking of your watch, and try and play the correct note lengths. You can try clapping the rhythm before you play.

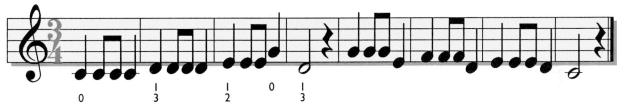

TONGUE TWISTERS

Notes played in rapid succession can be very exciting. Rapid notes can be achieved either by double-tonguing or by triple-tonguing. If you say the word "taka" quickly several times, you will produce a series of very fast sounds or notes. This is double-tonguing. If you say the word "tataka" quickly several times you get the same effect, but in groups of three. This is triple-tonguing. Trumpeter Wynton Marsalis (left) uses both methods of tonguing.

BREATHING

One of the most important things in trumpet playing is breathing. This may sound strange, because we are breathing all the time. But just as an engine provides power for a car, so your breath supply provides the power for your trumpet playing.

Hold your hand in front of your mouth and cough. You will notice that the air is pushed out quickly. Put your other hand on your stomach. Your stomach will feel as though it is being pushed upward. Now imagine blowing out all the candles on a birthday cake. Take a deep breath and push the air out as fast as you can. Make sure you can feel the "inward" movement in your stomach. Practice this until you become used to the amount of air you are breathing in and pushing out. Try blowing up a balloon as extra practice! Now position yourself where you can see a clock. Play the notes below, holding each one for as long as possible. Take a deep breath and try to keep the sound steady. Rest between each note and don't press too hard with your lips.

BAD HABITS

As you become more familiar with your trumpet, it is important to avoid bad habits. Always stand or sit correctly, keeping your shoulders and back straight. Hold the trumpet correctly. Use only the tips of your right hand fingers to press the valves down. Make sure you are forming your embouchure in the center of your mouth. Always start notes clearly and crisply.

PLAYING IN PUBLIC

When you eventually give your first performance, remember to take deep breaths, even before you play. Concentrate on the music, and don't get upset if you make a mistake — you are only human!

THOMAS HARPER (FATHER AND SON)

The two leading players of the natural trumpet in Britain during the 19th century were the two Thomas Harpers. Thomas Harper Sr. was in constant demand as a performer from about 1806, and played at all the principal concerts and festivals in London. Thomas Harper Jr., right, succeeded his father and became a big celebrity, too. Both musicians played a version of the natural trumpet called a "slide" trumpet.

SHARPS AND FLATS

The eight notes in the scale on page 71 are natural notes, the white notes on a piano. That scale is C major, because it starts on C. Scales that begin on other notes use sharps and flats, the black keys on the piano.

The sign for a sharp is shown on the left. A sharp raises the pitch of a note by a half step. A flat sign is shown below left. It lowers the pitch of a note by a half step. Sometimes sharps or flats appear in the "key signature" near the treble clef. They tell us the scale or key that the music is based on.

If no sharp or flat appears in the key signature, the key is C major. In the second line below, the key is G major, with F# in the key signature.

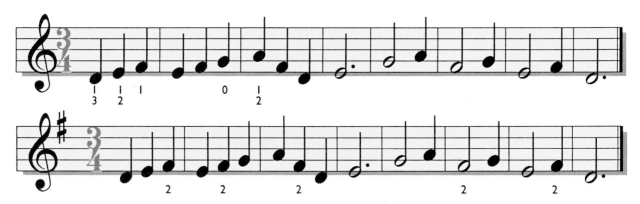

For every major key there is also a minor one. The first exercise below is in F major; the second is in D minor. Both have B♭ in the key signature.

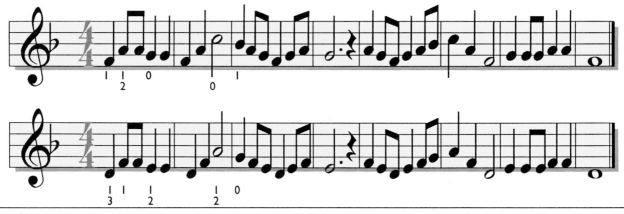

78

KEY SIGNATURES

Sharps or flats in the key signature do not appear in the music itself. The scales of D major and B minor have F# and C# in the key signature.

The scales of B♭ major and G minor both have B♭ and E♭ in their key signature. Remember to play these notes flat in the music itself.

Practice the exercises below, looking out for the key-signature. See if you can tell if they are written in a major or a minor key.

MAJOR AND MINOR

In the Middle Ages early forms of scales, or "modes," were used by choirs of monks in Christian churches. The monks would sing just one melody line, with no accompaniment. By the 13th century the music was sung in two or more parts; what we call "harmony" was born. Many modes gradually disappeared, leaving us by the 17th century with mainly the major and minor scales that we recognize today.

FINGER TECHNIQUE

Although there are only three valves on the trumpet, there are many different valve combinations. Some are very easy to play. Others are a little more difficult, and take longer to get used to. Move your fingers quickly and smoothly to a new valve combination, and make sure you don't sound a note while the valve is still half way down!

HAND MUSCLES

Hold your trumpet in your right hand as shown in the illustration below, and play the first and second valves alternately. You will find this change of fingering quite easy. If you try changing between the second and third valves you will find it much more difficult. This is because your third finger is rarely used on its own, and is much weaker than the others. The exercise below will help you to practice these difficult changes of fingering. Note that the music is in 3/4 time, with three quarter notes in a bar. The two sharps in the key signature indicate the key of D major or B minor. Play the music and see if you can tell which key it is.

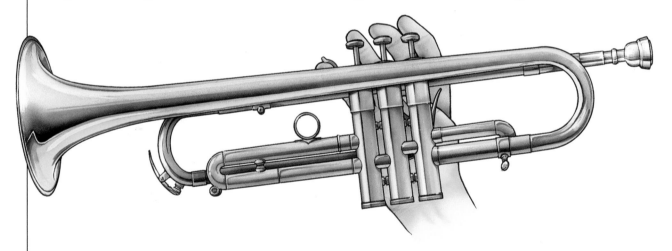

DOS AND DON'TS

Keep your right hand as relaxed as possible. Use the tips of the fingers to press down the valves. Never use the area underneath your knuckles. Always press the valve down quickly and smoothly. Press down combinations of valves together. Make sure the valves are down before you sound the note.

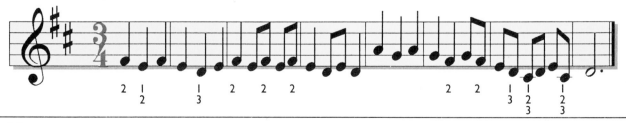

FIRST AND THIRD SLIDE

Some trumpets have moveable slides on their first and third valves. This is because some of the notes we play may be out of tune. By using these two slides it is possible to alter the tuning of the instrument when playing with these valves.

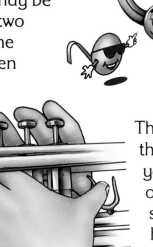

The illustration on the right shows the first valve slide, operated with your left thumb. The illustration on the left shows the third valve slide, operated with the left hand fourth finger. Play the exercises here without using the slides. Then play them again with both slides pulled out slightly — can you hear the difference?

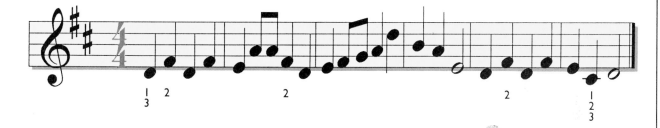

THE JAZZ TRUMPET

Since the beginning of this century, the trumpet has played a leading role in the development of jazz. Great jazz performers include Bix Biederbecke, a cornetist who made his impact in the 1920s. Dizzy Gillespie, right, helped develop the style of jazz in the 1940s called "Bebop." In the 1950s, trumpeter Miles Davis developed a more calm, or "cool," approach to jazz, influencing another great jazz trumpeter, Chet Baker.

PRACTICE ROUTINE

Regular practice of the trumpet is important. You don't have to spend many hours practicing — it is more useful to spend a short time every day. Because trumpeters use a very sensitive part of the body, the mouth, it is important to "warm up" properly.

REGULAR PRACTICE

Your daily practice routine should consist of a "warm-up," some scales, music set by your teacher, and any music that you really enjoy playing. Long notes are a good way of warming up, and improving your sound and stamina. Take a deep breath and see if you can hold a note for 16 seconds. If you find this is easy try 20, 30, or even 40 seconds!

Your long notes should be shaped as shown here, starting quietly, getting louder, and then becoming quieter again. The exercise below also gets louder and softer, as shown by the symbols like hairpins.

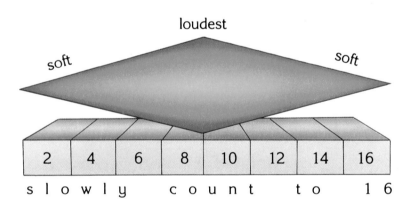

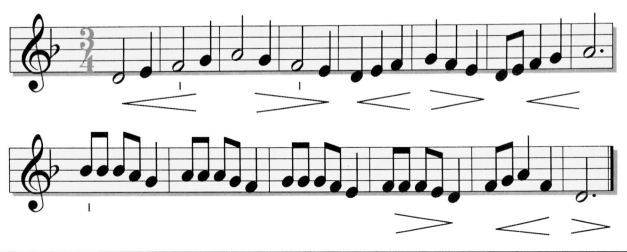

PLAYING A MELODY

The more you practice, the longer you will be able to play without becoming tired. As you improve, try to play melodies or pieces that are longer in length. Try the example below, in 3/4 time.

BRAHMS' LULLABY

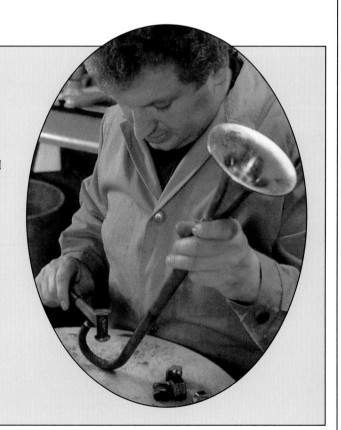

HOW A TRUMPET IS MADE

Traditionally, all trumpets were handmade by craftsmen, who shaped the trumpet bell by hand, beating it out on a steel form called a mandrel. The valves had to be cut to the correct length, then threaded, with the holes cut very carefully. The lengths of tubing to connect the bell and valves together were bent by heating the metal and hammering it into the correct shape. Today these processes are usually done mechanically, but there are some craftsmen, like Martin Lechner, right, who still use traditional methods.

PLAYING TOGETHER

So far, all the music you have played has been for one trumpet. The real fun, however, starts when you play with others. A piece of music for two players is called a duet. If you have a friend who is also learning the trumpet (or a cornet, or even a clarinet), try the following exercise. Make sure that the two parts are equal in sound.

PLAYING A DUET

When playing a duet, you have to listen to your own sound, and also to the sound your partner is making.

Make sure that you play notes together and that you are "in tune" with each other.

Place the music stand between the two players.

Count yourselves in. Try to start and finish at the same time.

CANON

Four or more musicians playing together are an "ensemble." The exercise below, a canon, can be played by up to six people. The players join in the music one by one, each person beginning the piece two bars after the person before. The large C indicates common (4/4) time.

MUTES

A mute is a device that is placed in or over the trumpet bell to soften, and to alter the sound. Three of the most common mutes are the "straight" mute, the "cup" mute, and the "harmon," or "wah-wah," mute. The "plunger" mute and "bucket" mute are sometimes used in jazz music to give a distinctive sound.

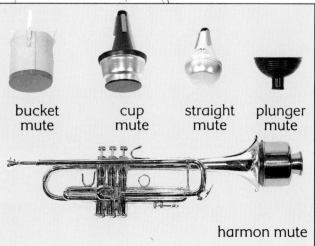

bucket mute   cup mute   straight mute   plunger mute

harmon mute

THE WORLD OF THE TRUMPET

The trumpet is a versatile instrument, used in many different kinds of music. It is heard in jazz, which was born at the start of the 20th century in New Orleans. It is also found in dance and military bands, and provides one of the most distinctive voices in the orchestra. Its relative, the cornet, is central to the brass band sound.

JAZZ BAND
French, Spanish, English, Italian, German, and Slav influences all merged in early jazz. In a jazz band, the cornet or trumpet, clarinet and trombone, may all provide the melody, and are accompanied by other stringed or brass instruments.

BIG BANDS
An important development of the "swing" era of the 1930s was the big band. It consisted of large sections of trumpets, trombones, and saxophones, with piano and drums adding to the melody and rhythm. It was through the big band that jazz became more popular.

THE ORCHESTRA

The brass section of the orchestra includes between two and five trumpets. It depends on how many the composer wanted to perform the music. In the 18th century, Mozart and Haydn wrote for only two trumpets. In the 19th and 20th centuries, Mahler and Stravinsky wrote for five or even six trumpets.

FANFARE TRUMPETS

Fanfare trumpets are used to great effect at ceremonial occasions. Their bright and exciting sound is due to their elongated shape. The flag or emblem that is attached to the bell is for visual effect only, and makes no difference to the sound produced.

MILITARY BANDS

The brass section of a military band includes trumpets, cornets, French horns, euphoniums, trombones, and tubas. The band will also contain a woodwind section, which includes oboes, flutes, clarinets, bassoons, and saxophones.

THE CORNET AND THE BRASS BAND

The cornet developed as a result of the invention of the valve, and became a favorite with performers. It has a prominent role in the brass band. Brass bands were first formed during the 19th century in England, as a pastime for coal miners. The brass band consists of about 25 musicians, playing cornets, flugel horns, tenor horns, euphoniums, and basses.

TRUMPET AND BRASS

Your trumpet is a member of a large family of trumpets, all named after the notes they correspond to on the piano. Your instrument is probably a B^b trumpet; there is also a C trumpet, a D trumpet, and so on. The higher the trumpet, the shorter the instrument will be.

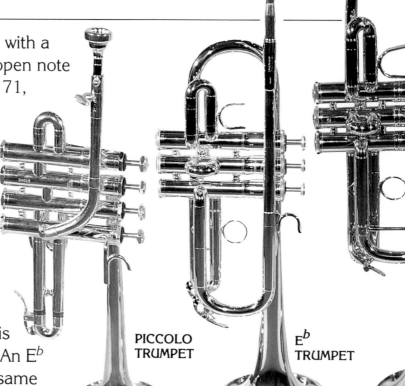

Try the following test with a piano. Play the first open note of the scale on page 71, your middle C, on your trumpet. Now play B^b on the piano, or ask someone to play it for you. The notes should sound the same on both instruments. Your C equals the piano's B^b, so your trumpet is called a B^b trumpet. An E^b trumpet playing the same open note would sound the same as E^b on the piano.

PICCOLO TRUMPET

E^b TRUMPET

C TRUMPET

ROTARY VALVE TRUMPET

The trumpets that are mostly used in the United States and Britain are known as piston trumpets. This name refers to the type of valve that is used in the instrument to produce a wider range of notes. In countries such as Germany and Austria, rotary valve trumpets are played instead. Rotary valves look similar to the valves used on French horns. Although they look different from piston trumpets, rotary valve trumpets are played in almost the same way.

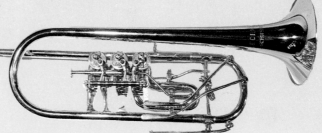

BRASS FAMILY

The **euphonium** (right) has a warm, deep, lyrical sound. The **trombone** (below) is the only modern brass instrument that uses a slide to produce a full range of notes.

The **sousaphone** was invented by John Philip Sousa for marching bands. The **tuba** (below) is another large member of the brass family. It was invented 150 years ago, for Russian military bands.

The **French horn** is a descendant of a hunting horn. It would measure over 16 feet (5 m) long if stretched out. The musician places one hand in the bell to improve the sound.

The **tenor horn** is used mainly in the brass band, where its warm, soft sound adds color. You can expect to see three or four tenor horns in many brass bands.

LOUIS ARMSTRONG

Louis Armstrong was one of the strongest influences in the history of jazz. He learned to play while at reform school (he had been arrested for firing blanks from a pistol in the street). He was soon in demand as a cornetist, and eventually formed his own bands. His influence on many musicians is widely acknowledged.

The Book
for
YOUNG
MUSICIANS

PIANO

AND KEYBOARDS

CONTENTS

INTRODUCING THE KEYBOARD

The keyboard, as its name implies, is a row of levers or keys placed above a wooden board. The keys sound the notes automatically, so the keyboard player does not have to worry about the pitch of the note. But, while most other musicians play only one note at a time, a keyboard player, using both hands, may have several notes to sound at once.

Keyboards do not all have the same number of keys or notes. Most pianos have eighty-eight. Other keyboards have less. But the keys are all arranged in the same way. The white notes form a continuous line. The black notes are separated by the white notes, and are arranged in groups of two or three.

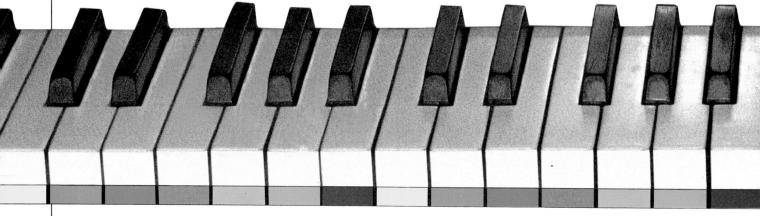

C | D | E | F | G | A | B | C | D | E | F | G | A | B

HIGH AND LOW

Bats emit very high-pitched sounds. Some of the noises they produce are so high that they cannot be detected by human ears.

Whales emit very low notes, which can be heard as throbs. The deep notes of an organ are also so low that only the throb of their vibrations is audible.

Low notes vibrate more slowly.

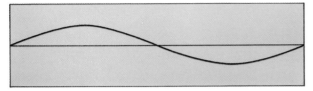

High notes vibrate more rapidly.

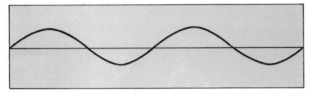

 **PITCH**

Sounds are vibrations. The more rapid they are, the higher is the "pitch" of a sound. Putting it another way, pitch is the highness or lowness of a note. It is measured by its "frequency" — the number of vibrations per second. The notes of a keyboard, from lowest to highest, go up from hundreds to thousands of vibrations per second.

Going from left to right as you sit at the keyboard, the keys or notes (white and black together) go up in pitch by a half tone, known as a "half step."

The white notes go up by a whole tone or by a half step. The black notes go up by a tone or by a tone and a half. Try out these "pitch intervals" yourself.

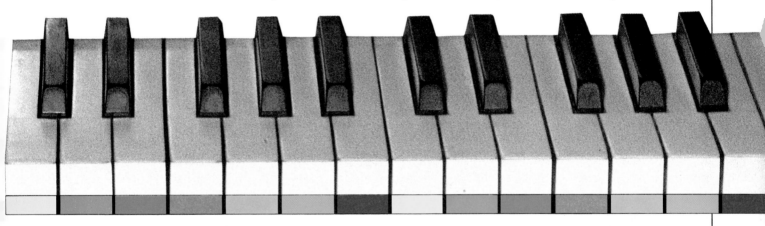

C D E F G A B C D E F G A B

THE HYDRAULIS

The earliest type of keyboard instrument was the hydraulis, or water organ, invented around 250 B.C. The hydraulis had pipes, and a small tank of water, which kept up the pressure of air. This instrument is the ancestor of the modern grand piano.

INSIDE YOUR PIANO

The piano is a stringed instrument. Each tightly stretched set of strings (one, two, or three to a note) is a different length. The longest sound the deepest notes, and as they get shorter, the notes become higher in pitch. Each key (lever) on the keyboard operates a little soft-headed hammer that strikes its own strings, making them vibrate and sound their note.

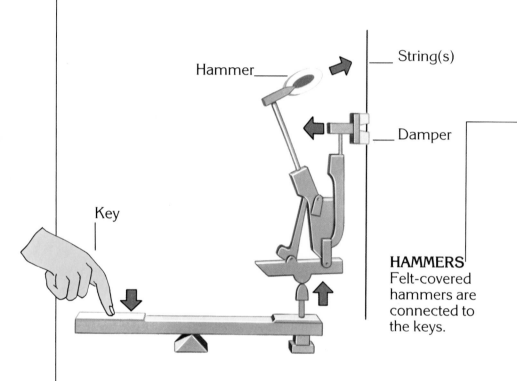

Hammer

Key

String(s)

Damper

HAMMERS
Felt-covered hammers are connected to the keys.

HOW A PIANO WORKS

The hammer mechanism is complicated. When you press a key, the hammer strikes the set of strings and bounces off again, so that the strings can vibrate. When you release the key, the damper connects with the strings and stops them from vibrating. An Italian craftsman invented the mechanism nearly 300 years ago. He called it the keyboard with "soft and loud," in Italian, *piano e forte*. That's why we call it the piano.

STRINGS
The strings, of copper or steel, are placed at an angle and across each other (overstrung) to save space, and to spread the tension of the strings across the frame.

SOUNDING BOARD
A metal sounding board amplifies the sound of the strings.

PARTS OF AN UPRIGHT PIANO

TUNING PEGS
Tuning pegs tighten or loosen the strings and keep them tuned to the right pitch.

DAMPERS
Dampers are pads that stop the strings from vibrating when the pianist takes his or her fingers off the keys.

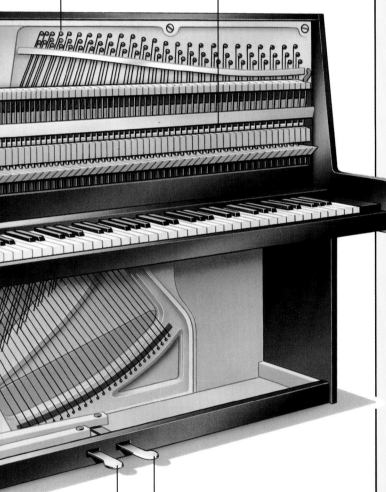

SOFT PEDAL
The "soft" pedal softens the note with the dampers.

SUSTAINING PEDAL
The "sustaining" pedal keeps the dampers off the strings, so that they vibrate longer.

DEVELOPMENT OF THE KEYBOARD

HARPSICHORD
The harpsichord is an older type of keyboard instrument. Its strings are plucked with a plectrum instead of being struck with a hammer.

SQUARE PIANO
An old "square piano" was in fact in the shape of a rectangle, not a true square. It had a shorter keyboard, and fewer strings, than a modern piano.

GRAND PIANO
The modern concert grand is a masterpiece of construction. Smaller grand pianos are called baby grands.

GETTING DOWN TO BUSINESS

The piano is a mechanical instrument, with many moving parts. We can think of the pianist as its driver. Just as the driver of a car sits in a certain position and uses hands and feet to control the vehicle, so the pianist must sit correctly and use arms, wrists, hands, and fingers in special ways to operate his or her instrument.

Keep your back straight. It's less tiring. Don't use an ordinary chair, which would restrict your movement. If the stool is too low, use a cushion.

POSTURE
Sit facing the note called Middle C, just above the lock for the keyboard lid. Your knees should be tucked just under the edge of the keyboard – then your hands will rest on the keyboard at just about the right height and distance from the rest of your body.

HANDS AND FINGERS
Place the fingers of each hand lightly on the middle of the white notes, not on the edge, and not too close to the black notes, as they might get stuck between them. Keep your hands fairly loose at the wrists. Keep your fingers slightly arched and relaxed.

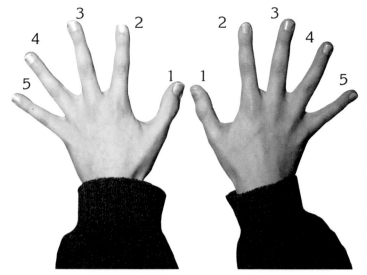

FINGERING

Fingering is about playing the notes with the most suitable fingers. It is a very important part of playing the piano. The fingers of each hand are numbered as shown. We sometimes speak of the thumb and fingers. But it is best to think of them all as a number from one to five, because that's how fingering is indicated on pieces of written music.

Middle C

FINDING MIDDLE C
Place your hands on the keyboard, with both thumbs on Middle C. The fingering of left and right hands works the opposite way around – an obvious point, but an important one.

CARING FOR YOUR PIANO

Have your piano tuned at least once a year. Keep the keys clean with a sponge or cloth moistened with warm, soapy water.

Keep a cup or bowl of water by the piano, if it is in a warm, dry room.

Don't place the piano by a radiator. The heat may crack part of the frame. Don't place your piano in strong sunlight, which would be bad for the polish or varnish.

Don't put drinks by the keyboard or on top of the piano.

PLAYING A SCALE

The word "scale" comes from the Italian word *scala*, meaning "step." Scales are steps of notes running up and down the keyboard. Playing scales is the best way to learn good fingering, and tone up the muscles in your hands.

5 4 3 2 1

1 2 3 4 5

FIVE-FINGER EXERCISE
With the left hand, start with the fifth finger on the note shown and go up five white notes to Middle C, one finger per note, and down again. With the right hand, start with the first finger (thumb) on Middle C and go up five white notes, one finger per note, and down again. Repeat this until you find it easy.

LEFT-HAND SCALE
Start with the fifth finger on the note eight white notes down from Middle C. Come up the scale one note at a time. When you reach the thumb, bring the third finger over on the next note, and complete the scale up to C.

Going up, when you reach the thumb, bring the third finger over.

1

3

2

CAMILLE SAINT-SAËNS

The French composer Camille Saint-Saëns wrote *Carnival of the Animals*, which includes pieces about elephants, a donkey, a swan, a tortoise, and fish in an aquarium. There is also a light-hearted piece called "Pianists." In it, two pianists pound up and down the keyboard, as though practicing their scales. Listen for it.

Saint-Saëns was a famous organist and pianist. As well as *Carnival of the Animals* he composed operas, symphonies, and concertos. He died in 1921, at the age of 86.

     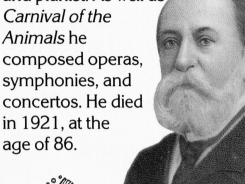

RIGHT-HAND SCALE

Start with the first finger (the thumb) on Middle C. Bring the thumb under the third finger, and complete the upward scale of eight white notes, one finger per note. Coming down, bring the third finger over the thumb to complete the scale back to C.

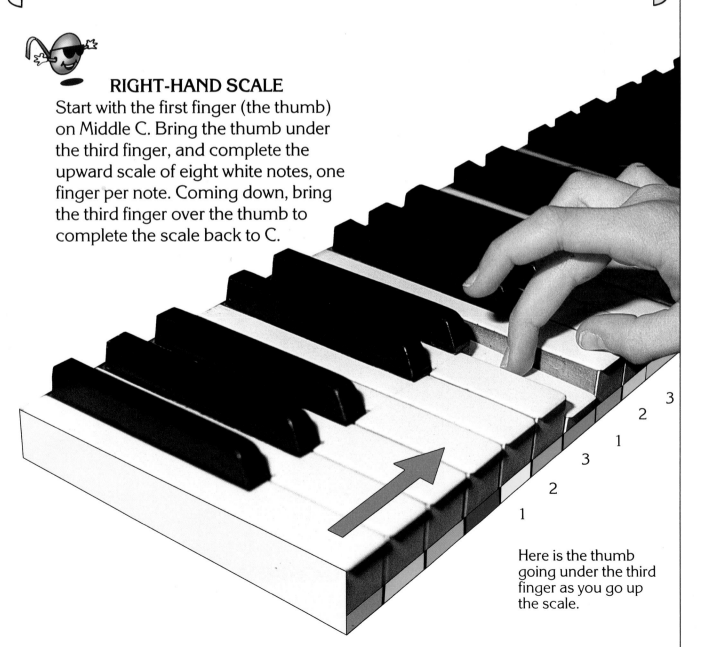

Here is the thumb going under the third finger as you go up the scale.

READING THE DOTS

Notation is the name given to written music. It is the equivalent of the letters and words of written language. Notation has to indicate the pitch of the notes in a piece of music (how high or low the notes are), as well as the rhythm of the music. The next pages will explore both these aspects of notated music.

NAMING THE NOTES

The pitch of notes is indicated by five lines called a staff. Whether notes are placed on, between, above, or below these lines tells us their pitch. The notes are named after the letters A to G. On the right you can see an easy way of remembering the notes on and between the lines for the left hand.

On the lines: Good Boys Deserve Fun Always.

Between the lines: All Cows Eat Grass.

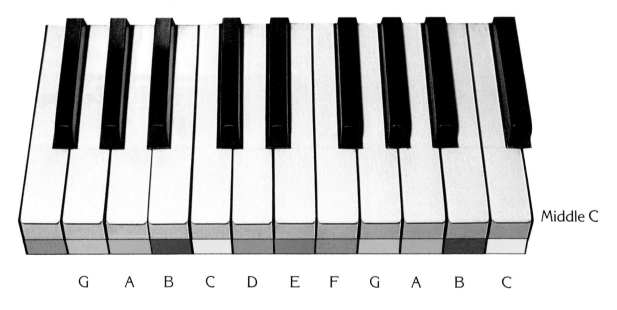

| G | A | B | C | D | E | F | G | A | B | C |

Middle C

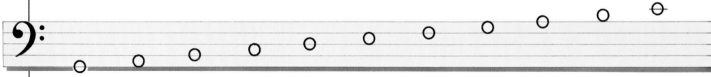

The bass clef sign (above) indicates the pitch range of the notes played by the left hand.

Above are the main notes for the left hand shown on the keyboard, and in notation.

The notes are called by the letters of the alphabet from A to G. After G the letters begin again.

THE HISTORY OF NOTATION

The system of notation we use today dates back nearly a thousand years. Early examples from the 10th and 11th centuries show staff lines, with notes written on or between them. Clef signs sometimes appear at the beginning of the music. Some early manuscripts have different symbols for notes of different lengths.

MORE NOTES TO LEARN

Here are the main notes for the right hand shown in notation, and on the keyboard, with their names as letters.

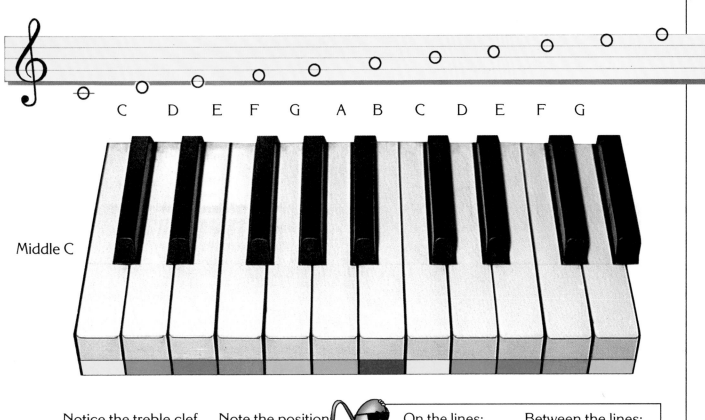

C D E F G A B C D E F G

Middle C

Notice the treble clef sign this time, which indicates the pitch range of notes for the right hand to play.

Note the position of Middle C in the treble clef. Look to see where it was in the bass clef.

On the lines: Elephants Go Breaking Down Fences.

Between the lines: the names of the notes spell FACE.

On the right you can see a simple way of remembering the notes on and between the lines in the treble clef.

ADDING THE BEAT

Rhythm drives a piece of music along. Clapping your hands to music is a good way of finding its rhythm, that is, its beat. This beat is usually divided into regular sections, called bars, or measures. We speak of the rhythm of a piece of music as so many beats to the bar.

TIME VALUE OF NOTES
Notes may last for a longer or shorter time, as long as they keep to the rhythm. The note shown here that lasts longest is the whole note. Reading from left to right, each of the other notes is half the duration, or time value, of the one before.

One whole note   Two half notes   Four quarter notes

BEATS TO THE BAR
Music is divided into bars or measures. The number and value of the beats in each bar is the time signature, which appears beside the clef sign. 4/4 time has four quarter notes to every bar, or the equivalent made up in notes of other time values.

TEMPO
Tempo means the pace, or speed, of the music, as distinct from its rhythm. Common tempo indications, which are all Italian words, are *adagio* (slow), *andante* (fairly slow), *allegro* (fast) and *presto* (very fast). These directions appear at the beginning of the piece of music.

See how the notes fit into rhythms of so many beats to each bar.

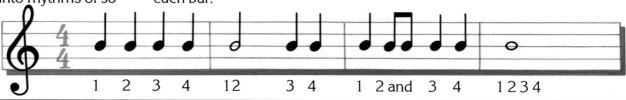

MORE TIME SIGNATURES

3/4 time and 6/8 time are two other time signatures which are often used in music. 3/4 time has three quarter notes to every bar, or the equivalent in other notes. 6/8 time has six eighth notes to every bar, or the equivalent.

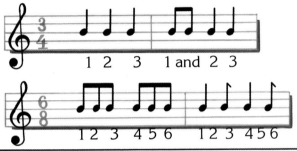

1 2   3   1 and 2 3

1 2 3   4 5 6   1 2 3   4 5 6

Try clapping to rhythms above.

Eight eighth-notes

RHYTHM AND DANCE

The waltz, in 3/4 rhythm, is the most popular dance of all time. It began in Germany and Austria about 170 years ago. One of the most successful composers of waltzes was Johann Strauss II. Strauss lived in Vienna and wrote many popular waltzes, such as "The Blue Danube" and "Tales from the Vienna Woods."

Rock and roll is in 4/4 rhythm. It started in the 1950s as a kind of up tempo, speeded-up blues. Elvis Presley was one of its greatest stars. Much of today's rock music is based on rock and roll.

MORE EXERCISES

On pages 98-99, you played a scale of eight notes (an octave) in boths hands. Scales are one kind of exercise for practicing fingering and for strengthening fingers, hands, and wrists. Other kinds of exercises also strengthen the same muscles. This page has some exercises you can try.

BROKEN CHORDS

Broken chords involve playing the notes of chords as individual notes. This exercise stretches your fingers and gets you used to playing notes that are farther apart on the keyboard.

Here is the notation for a sequence of broken chords for the left hand. Follow the fingering below.

On the opposite page you can see the same sequence of notes for the right hand to play.

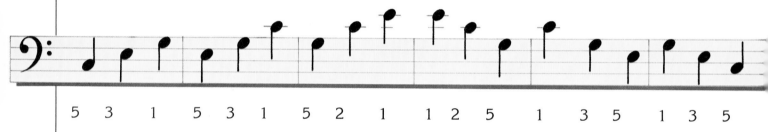

5   3   1   5   3   1   5   2   1   1   2   5   1   3   5   1   3   5

PLAYING CHORDS

Chords are two or more notes of different pitch sounded together. Try these chords of three notes: two for the left hand and two for the right. The notes are shown on the keyboard and in the notation.

CHROMATIC SCALE

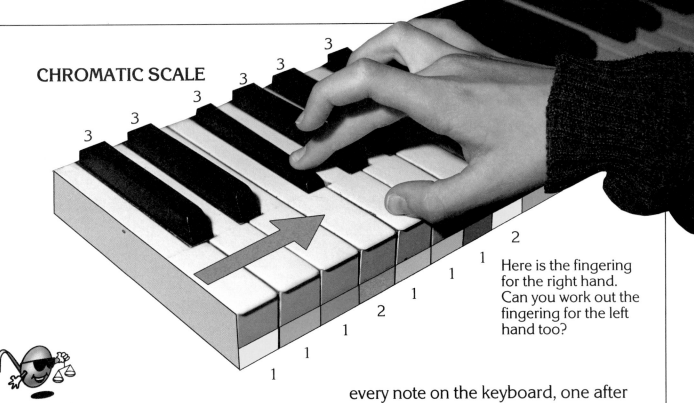

Here is the fingering for the right hand. Can you work out the fingering for the left hand too?

This exercise involves playing black notes as well as white ones, for in the chromatic scale you must play every note on the keyboard, one after the other. The scale uses a special fingering, with only the thumb (no 1) and the next two fingers (2 and 3).

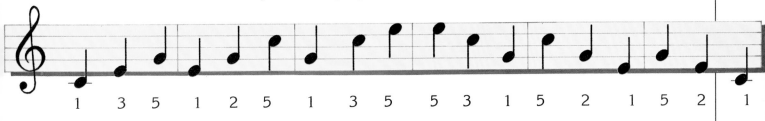

1 3 5 1 2 5 1 3 5 5 3 1 5 2 1 5 2 1

FRANZ LISZT

The most famous pianist of all time was the Hungarian Franz Liszt (1811–86). As a young man Liszt was very good looking, and when he started to play, young women sometimes fainted or screamed, as some fans do at rock concerts today. During Liszt's long life, pianos were made bigger and stronger, which inspired him to write a new kind of piano music. Much of this is extremely difficult to play. Listen to Liszt's *Hungarian Rhapsodies*, his exciting arrangements of old Hungarian gypsy songs and dances, and to his famous *Liebestraum* (or *Dream of Love*).

INTRODUCING SHARPS AND FLATS

The scale of eight white notes you played on pages 98-99 started and ended on the note C. It was the scale of C major. To play the same kind of scale starting and ending on a different note is more complicated. These pages introduce the scale of G major, for left and right hands. The fingering is the same as for the scale of C.

G MAJOR IN THE LEFT HAND

Below are the notes for the left hand, going up. Notice the sharp sign on the staff line for the note F.

Instead of playing the white note F, play the adjacent black note of F sharp.

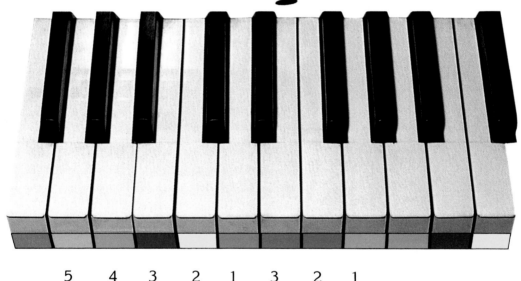

5	4	3	2	1	3	2	1
G	A	B	C	D	E	F#	G

KEY SIGNATURES
The F# in the "key signature" near the clef tells you the key is G. The sharp is not marked again in the music.

SHARPS AND FLATS
The sharp sign (#) tells you to raise the pitch of a note by a half-tone. The flat sign (b) tells you to lower the pitch of a note by a half-tone.

G MAJOR IN THE RIGHT HAND

Here is the same scale for the right hand, going up. Once again, notice the position of the sharp sign, on the staff line for the note F (this time in the treble clef). The sign tells you to play the note F sharp. As in the left hand, the fingering is the same as for the scale of C major, up and down.

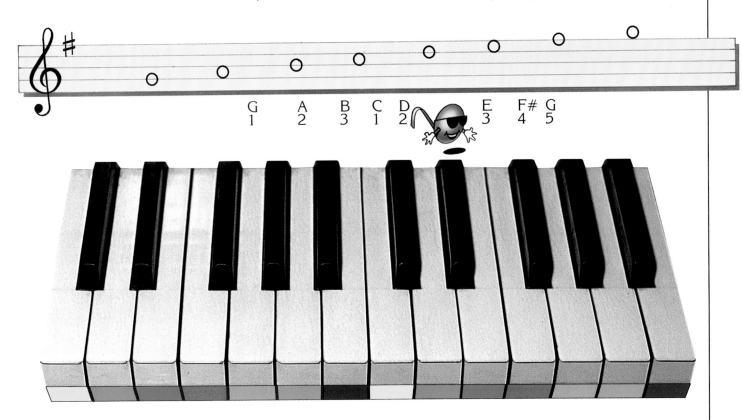

G	A	B	C	D	E	F#	G
1	2	3	1	2	3	4	5

FREDERIC CHOPIN

Frederic Chopin (1810–49) wrote a piano piece known as the "Black Key Etude," because the right-hand part is all on the black notes. A study (in French *etude*) is a piece intended as an exercise, though Chopin's piano studies are also beautiful pieces of music. Chopin, who was Polish, was both a great pianist and a great composer of piano music. Several other pieces by Chopin have popular nicknames, including the "Raindrop Prelude," the "Minute Waltz," the "Winter Wind Etude," and the "Butterfly Etude."

MAJOR AND MINOR

You have already met the scales of C major and G major. You can play a major scale starting on any of the white or black notes (depending on how many sharps or flats are included). Minor scales are organized in a different way, and have quite a different sound to them.

A MINOR

Minor scales can also start and end on any of the white and black notes. Below is the notation and fingering for the scale of A minor for the left and right hands going up and down. You'll see that the treble clef part appears above the bass clef part. This is the normal order for the right- and left-hand parts in written music.

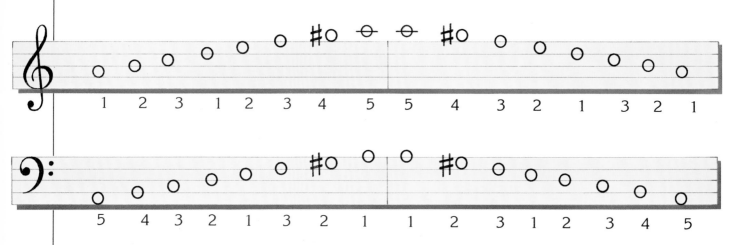

In this scale the note G is "accidentally" sharpened (see page 109). You must play G sharp every time you come to it.

The "soft" and "sustaining" pedals are used to make the piano sound softer or louder, or sustain (hold onto) notes.

ACCIDENTALS

Accidentals are any notes that are sharpened or flattened, in addition to the sharps or flats that are indicated in the key signature. In the scale of A minor, the note G is "accidentally" sharpened. And in the scale of E minor (below) the note D is "accidentally" sharpened – in addition to the note F, which is already sharpened by the key signature.

NATURALS

The "natural" sign (shown on the right) looks quite like the sign for a sharp. But beware, this sign means that the instruction to sharpen or flatten a note has been canceled. If the note F has been sharpened, but the composer now wants you to play the white note F, he puts a natural sign beside it. You must play F natural, not F sharp.

E MINOR

Here is the notation for the scale of E minor for the left and right hands going up and down. Notice the F sharp in the key signature. The fingering is the same for this scale as for the other scales you have met.

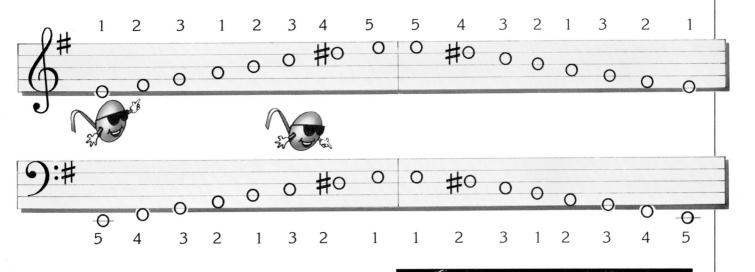

The note F has been sharpened in the key signature. Play F sharp every time you come to it.

The note D is "accidentally" sharpened. Play D sharp every time you come to it.

Japanese pianist Mitsuko Uchida is renowned for her performances today.

PLAYING MELODIES

Now you are ready to play some real melodies. These two pieces are written in the treble clef, because it is usually the right hand that plays the melody in piano music. New points about notation are explained on the opposite page.

ODE TO JOY

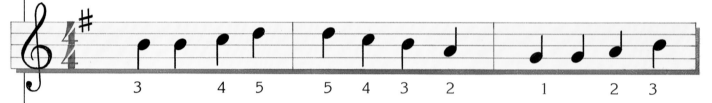

3   4 5   5 4 3 2   1   2 3

3 2   3   4 5   5 4 3 2

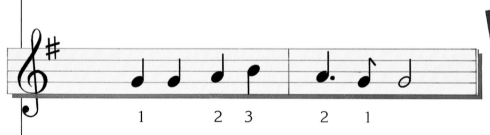

1   2 3   2 1

The German composer Ludwig van Beethoven (1770–1827) wrote dramatic and exciting piano music.

The "Ode to Joy" is the melody from the last movement of Beethoven's Ninth ("Choral") Symphony. It is the national anthem of the European Community. This arrangement is in G major, with F sharp in the key signature.

RESTS

A rest is a silent beat in a bar of music. Different rest symbols correspond to the different kinds of notes, and show how long the silence should be.

whole note   half note

quarter note   eighth note

DOTTED NOTES AND TIES

A dot after a note increases the time value of the note by a half. A tie connects two notes of the same pitch. Play them as one long note.

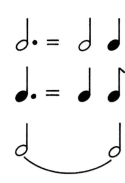

PLAISIR D'AMOUR

●A dot after this half note means the two beats of the note are increased to three.

Play two tied notes as one long note, adding their time value together.

Notice the B flat in the key signature (F major). Remember to play B flat here.

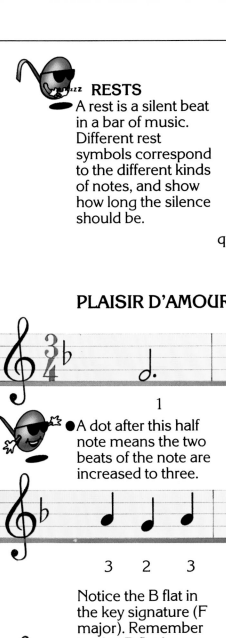

"Plaisir d'amour" was written about two hundred years ago by Martini il Tedesco (Martini the German). Elvis Presley and folk-singer Joan Baez have both sung versions of it. This arrangement is in the key of F major (with a B flat in the key signature).

111

BOTH HANDS NOW

Now is the time to play a piece with both hands. Practice the parts separately before you try to play them together. Later you will be able to read and play both the right- and left-hand parts at the same time.

GREENSLEEVES

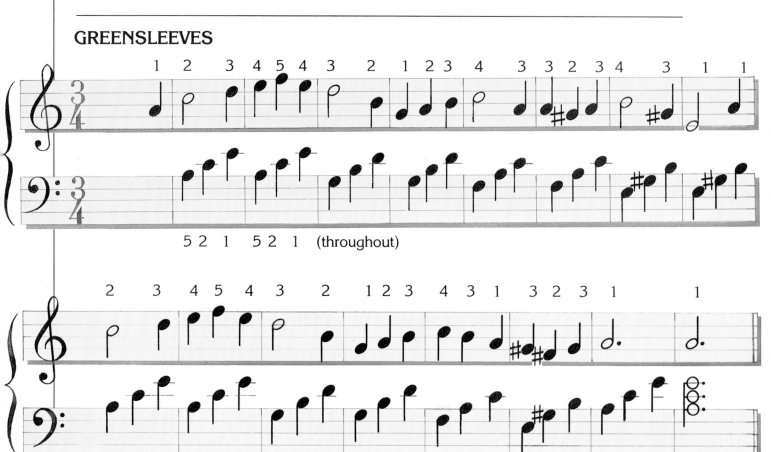

GREENSLEEVES

The old English folk song "Greensleeves" dates back to the time of Shakespeare, or even earlier. It is an early love ballad – a form still popular among musicians today, including keyboard player Stevie Wonder (right). This arrangement is in the key of A minor, with no sharps or flats in the key signature; but there are some accidental sharps. The rhythm has been simplified slightly.

TWELVE-BAR BLUES

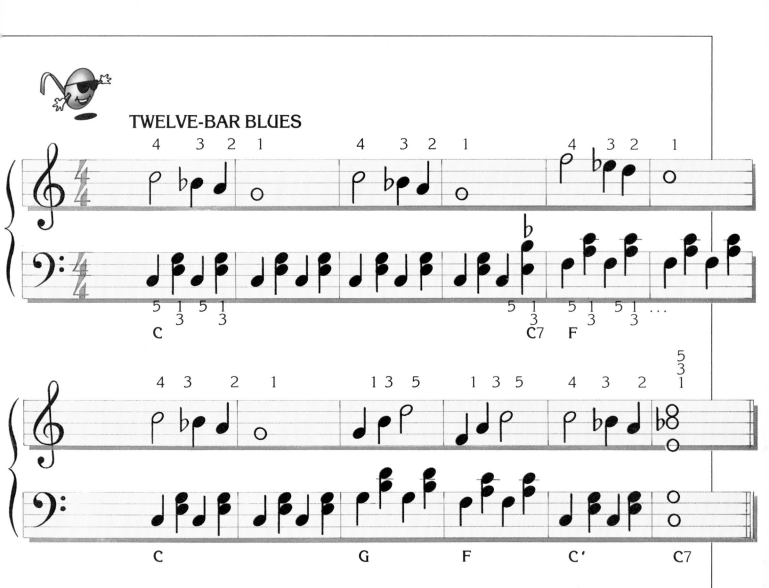

THE BLUES

Blues was originally a kind of folk music that originated among American black people. The twelve-bar blues is the classic form. Much of the music of jazz, leading to rock and roll, started with the blues. The American composer and musician W.C. Handy (right) is often called the "father of the blues." He wrote the famous "St. Louis Blues" and "Basin Street Blues."

TWELVE-BAR BLUES

Notice the accidental flat notes in the piece above. The rhythm of the melody has been kept simple; see if you can "jazz it up" a bit. You'll see, too, that chord symbols have been added. These are great fun; ask in your library or in a music store for a book showing how they work.

THE WORLD OF THE PIANO

The piano is the most popular of all instruments, because it can play melody and harmonies together. More people play the piano than any other instrument, and more well-known music has been written for the piano than for any other instrument. The piano is also very versatile – you can see some of its many roles on these pages.

PIANO AND ORCHESTRA

The use of the piano as an instrument in the orchestra dates back to the beginning of the 20th century. Before that, the piano was used as a concerto instrument only. (A concerto is a composition usually for a solo instrument and orchestra.) The composer Igor Stravinsky was one of the first to use the piano in the orchestra. Other composers have followed his example.

PIANO QUARTET

The piano is perhaps best known as a solo or concerto instrument. But great music has also been written for the piano quartet (piano plus violin, viola and cello) and for the piano trio (piano plus violin and cello).

PLAYER PIANO

You don't have to be able to play the piano to work a player piano! This is a mechanical piano, worked by a roll of paper with thousands of little holes, or perforations, in it. It was popular in the days before records.

HONKY-TONK PIANO

Honky-tonk music is played in saloons, clubs and some dance halls. Famous American boogie-woogie pianists such as Clarence "Pine Top" Smith and Charlie "Cow Cow" Davenport played in honky-tonk saloons and halls 60–70 years ago.

JAZZ PIANO

Jazz and dance bands, such as Louis Armstrong's Hot Five (right), nearly always have a piano. Two of the greatest American band leaders, "Duke" Ellington and "Count" Basie, were pianists. They conducted their bands seated at the piano.

PREPARED PIANO

The "prepared piano" was the idea of American composer and musical thinker John Cage. Cage inserted objects such as pencils and rubber bands between the strings, or placed them over the strings, to change the whole sound of the piano. He has written a "Concerto for Prepared Piano." Cage has written (or thought of) many other extraordinary pieces of music, involving the use of tape recorders, whistles, radios, and even bottles of water!

THE KEYBOARD FAMILY

The keyboard was one of the most important musical inventions. The system of scales and keys we know today is largely based on it. The keyboard has been used in a wide variety of instruments besides the piano and the older harpsichord, just some of which are shown here.

French musician Jean-Michel Jarre (above right) pioneered the use of synthesizers and electronic sounds.

ELECTRIC KEYBOARDS

Electric organs and pianos are played very like an ordinary piano, but the sounds, like those of the synthesizer, are electronic. These instruments are very popular with jazz musicians and pop groups.

ELECTRIC ORGAN

Electric organs began to appear in movies and theaters in the 1920s. They were technically very advanced for their time, and could produce many extraordinary sounds. Visually these organs made a dramatic impact on audiences, as they rose up from the pit in front of the screen or stage during intervals in performances, with their many lights flashing.

SYNTHESIZER

Synthesizers (above) generate electronic signals which are fed though amplifiers and speakers. These signals can produce many different sounds.

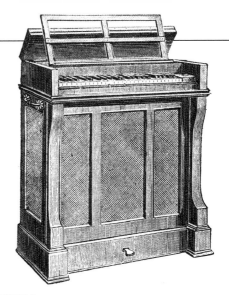

CELESTA

The keyboard of a celesta plays a set of tuned metal bars inside the instrument. Tchaikovsky's "Dance of the Sugar Plum Fairy" is written for it.

ACCORDION

The accordion (right) is a kind of portable organ, with a keyboard down one side. Learning to play the keyboard at this angle takes a great deal of practice.

CHURCH ORGAN

A large church or concert organ (right) often has three or four keyboards (known as "manuals"), plus a pedal keyboard, which is played with the feet. There are also a variety of "stops" – knobs or handles that the organist pulls out or pushes in to select whole groups or sets of pipes. All these devices are needed because many organs have a large number of pipes, with a range of different sound qualities, as well as notes of different pitch. Electric organs which were used in movies or theaters are now sometimes used in churches. The organ shown on the opposite page is reused in this way.

COMPOSERS

The following list of famous composers have written music for piano, flute, trumpet, or violin. Some have written for all of these. The composers below span the Baroque (c.1600-1750), Classical (c.1750-1820), Romantic (c.1820-1900) periods as well as the new developments of the 20th century and present day. The Baroque period featured very elaborate, rich music, with new forms of vocal work. The Classical period emphasized a balance and elegance in the different sections of a piece of music. In the Romantic period composers believed music should be highly imaginative and emotional. The 1900s has seen many developments, such as new ideas in harmony, and popular music such as jazz.

BACH, Johann Sebastian (1685-1750)
A very famous German composer of the Baroque period. He was also a choirmaster and a brilliant organist. He wrote sonatas, suites, and cantatas and other orchestral works for many different instruments. His fugues (pieces in which the notes of a theme follow themselves up and down the keyboard) are particularly famous. Bach wrote much music for the organ, including "chorales" based on old German hymn tunes. He also wrote many works for the flute, including "The Musical Offering," written for Frederick the Great, and the B minor suite.

J.S.Bach

BEETHOVEN, Ludwig van (1770-1827)
One of the greatest composers in history. A German composer who was revolutionary in that he broke away from the tradition of writing religious music, and wrote music to be listened to for its own sake. He wrote many dramatic concertos and sonatas for the piano. From the age of 30, Beethoven's hearing began to fail, and some of his greatest works were composed when he was deaf. His violin concerto, a powerful piece, opens with four ominous drumbeats. The virtuoso violin concerto went on to become a very popular form in the course of the 19th century.

BERLIOZ, Hector (1803-69)
A French composer who wrote his violin concerto in memory of a young girl. It begins with just the four open strings.

BERNSTEIN, Leonard (1918-91)
An American composer and

BARTOK, Béla (1881-1945)
Hungarian composer who developed a national style based on the folk and gypsy music of his country. This is clear in his writing for the violin.

conductor whose music is inspired by jazz, Broadway musicals, and traditional Jewish music.

BIEDERBECKE, Bix (1903-1931)
Jazz pianist, cornet-player, and composer, who wrote "Singin' the Blues" and "In A Mist."

BIRTWISTLE, Harrison (b.1934)
A present-day English composer who has written concertos for trumpet with orchestral accompaniment.

Bix Biederbecke

BOULEZ, Pierre (b.1925)
A French composer and conductor whose sonatine contains modern techniques which give the flute a wide range of expression.

BRAHMS, Johann (1833-97)
A great German composer, who has been regarded as the leading composer of Romantic symphonies, concertos, and chamber music. When he wrote his famous violin concerto it was first thought to be unplayable. It was called a concerto "not for but against the violin."

BRITTEN, Benjamin (1913-76)
A versatile English composer who has written work for particular performers, and for amateurs and children, such as "The War Requiem."

BRUCH, Max (1838-1920)
A German composer who wrote two very popular violin concertos.

BYRD, William (1543-1623)
An English composer

Claude Debussy

known for his religious music, and for being one of the first composers of keyboard music. The Renaissance period, between 1400 and 1600, saw the beginning of the great age of keyboard music. Byrd composed for the virginal, a stringed keyboard instrument similar to the harpsichord.

CHAMINADE, Cécile Louise Stephanie (1857-1944)
French composer and pianist whose flute concerto has a delightful Hollywood-style opening and furious technical sections.

CHOPIN, Frédéric (1810-49)
One of the greatest pianist-composers who wrote for solo piano. He discovered a new, poetic character

for the new 19th century piano.

COPLAND, Aaron (1900-91)
American composer who wrote several film, ballet, and theatre scores.

CORELLI, Arcangelo (1653-1713)
A celebrated violinist and teacher, who was the first to write specifically for the violin. But even the hardest pieces he wrote seem quite easy by modern technical standards.

COUPERIN, François (1668-1733)
Couperin composed music for harpsichord and organ. Today this music is often played on the piano.

DEBUSSY, Claude (1862-1918)
A French pianist-composer. By the 19th century grand pianos had a beautiful sound and touch, and Debussy was very inspired by this. He created musical "impressions" of natural phenomena like rain, sunlight, and snow. His "L'apres-midi d'un faune" begins with a haunting flute solo, and his "Syrinx"

is possibly the best-known solo piece for the flute.

DELIUS, Frederick (1862-1934)
English composer who is famous for his rich harmonies and romantic music.

DVORAK, Antonin (1841-1904)
Czech composer whose symphonies, concertos and chamber music are colorful, and

George Gerschwin

dramatic, reflecting the character of Czech music.

ELGAR, Sir Edward William (1857-1934)
A British violinist and composer of the Romantic tradition. He wrote many orchestral works, including "The Enigma Variations."

His violin concerto is also famous.

FAURE, Gabriel (1854-1924)
French composer and teacher of many fine songs and chamber works. He was a great harmonist who wrote very poetic music.

GERSHWIN, George (1898-1937)
American composer of songs, revues and musical comedies. He brought popular music into the concert hall and opera house, with his "Rhapsody in

George Handel

Blue," "American in Paris," and "Porgy and Bess."

GLASS, Phillip (b.1937)
American composer and leading member of the "minimalist school" by which a composer uses a small number of notes or chords in a piece. He has written an opera called "Einstein on the Beach."

GLUCK, Christoph von (1714-87) Gluck is loved by flutists for his beautiful "Dance of the Blessed Spirits" from his opera "Orfeo ed Euridice."

GREIG, Edvard (1843-1907)
The first Norwegian composer to win a worldwide reputation. He was inspired by folk music and was a great harmonic innovator who prepared the way for later 20th century composers. He wrote many small pieces for piano as well as his famous piano concerto and the music for "Peer Gynt."

HANDEL, George (1685-1759)
Handel was born in Germany but moved to England where he became a very famous composer. He wrote many beautiful oratorios, cantatas, operas, and other orchestral works.

Scott Joplin

HAYDN, Joseph (1732-1809),
An Austrian composer, who composed more than 100 symphonies. He also wrote a magnificent concerto for the "keyed trumpet" a new invention of the early nineteenth century.

HINDEMITH, Paul (1895-1963)
German viola-player and composer who wrote energetic sonatas for the flute.

HOLST, Gustav (1874-1934)
English composer and teacher who began his career as a trombonist. His works include the brilliant orchestral suite, *The Planets,* and chamber opera *Savitri.*

HUMMEL, Johann (1778-1837)
Hummel wrote a new concerto for the trumpet, following experimentation by manufacturers with valves and with different types of trumpet.

IBERT, Jacques (1890-1962)
Ibert wrote a new type of music for the 20th century valved trumpet and piano.

JOPLIN, Scott (1868-1917)
Jazz was the music of black Americans; throughout this century jazz has inspired many brilliant, mostly black pianists. Joplin is remembered for his piano pieces, called "rags."

KUHLAU, Daniel Friedrich (1786-1832)
Kuhlau was an exceptional flute player and composer during the time when a flute was extremely popular.

Friedrich Kuhlau

MAHLER, Gustav (1860-1911)
An Austrian composer and conductor of the Romantic period, who wrote nine symphonies and many song-cycles which are known for their emotional expression.

MATINI, Bohuslav (1890-1959)
Matini wrote much celebrated music for trumpet with piano accompaniment.

Gustav Mahler

MAXWELL-DAVIES, Peter (b.1934)
An English composer who was influenced by medieval techniques and has written for the trumpet and full orchestra.

MENDELSSOHN, Felix ((1809-47)
German composer who combined poetic imagination with a pure style. His violin concerto is very famous.

MOZART, Wolfgang Amadeus (1756-1791)
A child prodigy who gave concerts all over Europe from the age of five. He wrote his five violin concertos in one year, when he was 19. He also wrote much chamber music that includes the violin. His flute quartets and concertos are very popular. His last opera was "The Magic Flute." Its hero, Tamino, is protected on his quest by the flute given to him by the Queen of the Night. Mozart wrote sonatas and other music for harpsichord or piano. Mozart could play the harpsichord at the age of three, and gave concerts all over Europe. Later he wrote the first great piano concertos.

MUSSORGSKY, Modeste (1839-81)
Russian composer who is known for his rugged and individual style. His masterpiece. "Boris Godunov," is recognised as one of the most original and completely Russian of all operas.

NEILSEN, Carl (1865-1931)
Denmark's greatest

Felix Mendelssohn

and most influential composer who wrote six great orchestral symphonies, and some of the best known 20th century concertos for the flute.

PAGANINI, Niccolo (1782-1840)
Italian violinist who was dramatic on stage and raised solo playing to brilliant technical height. He was also a serious composer. His 24 'Caprices' for solo violin are standard works for players today.

PROKOFIEV, Sergei (1891-1953)
Prokofiev was another child prodigy, who wrote his first opera when he was nine years old. His work "Peter and the Wolf" provides a guide to the instruments in the orchestra. He also wrote two violin concertos.

PUCCINI, Giacomo (1858-1924)
The most famous and successful of 20th century Italian opera composers. A fine harmonist and melodist, he knew how to obtain great dramatic effects for his operas. They are still popular today.

PURCELL, Henry (1659-95)
The greatest and most versatile of English composers. He was organist of Westminster Abbey and main composer of ceremonial and state music. He also wrote for the theater.

RACHMANINOV, Sergei (1873-1943)
Russian composer who is most famous for his three piano concertos. They are in the romantic tradition and are often somber in tone.

W. A. Mozart

RAVEL, Maurice (1875-1937) Like Debussy, Ravel created musical impressions of natural phenomena for the orchestra, and much beautiful music for the piano and trumpet.

RIMSKY-KORSAKOV, Nickolai (1844-1908) One of the most distinguished of the Russian nationalist composers. He edited for performance many

Sergei Prokofiev

of the unfinished scores of Borodin and Mussorgsky.

SCARLATTI, Domenico (1685-1732) Italian composer and harpsichordist who wrote many sonatas which are now played on the piano.

SCHUBERT, Franz (1797-1828) An Austrian composer who produced masterpieces in every field except opera.

SCHUMANN, Robert (1810-56) German composer, who although a Romantic, was very much influenced by Bach.

SHOSTAKOVICH, Dimitri (1906-75) Russian composer who won early attention with his first symphony, written while he was still a student. He wrote two violin concertos.

SIBELIUS, Jean (1865-1957) Finland's greatest composer, who wrote a famous violin concerto.

SOUSA, John Philip (1854-1933) American bandmaster who toured the world with his own virtuoso band. He is remembered for his exuberant and inventive marches.

STRAVINSKY, Igor (1882-1971) A Russian composer,

Richard Wagner

known for his Russian inventiveness, who wrote one violin concerto.

TARTINI, Giuseppe (1692-1770) A baroque violinist-composer. His famous "Devil's Trill" sonata is one of the first virtuoso violin pieces. He claimed that the devil had shown him how to play it in a dream.

TCHAIKOVSKY, Peter Ilyich (1840-93) A muchloved Russian composer of the Romantic period who wrote great orchestral works and ballets and a violin concerto.

TORELLI, Giuseppe (1658-1709) Torelli was one of the first to develop concertos and sinfonias for trumpets prior to the invention of the valve.

VAUGHAN WILLIAMS, Ralph (1872-1958) English composer who was inspired by folk music. He wrote much for amateurs, and was regarded as the fatherfigure of English music from the 1930s until the time of his death.

VERDI, Guiseppe (1813-1901) Very popular Italian opera composer. He wrote 24 operas over 50 years.

VIVALDI, Antonio (1678-1741) Italian priest, violinist and composer, wrote church music, symphonies, and concertos for strings and wind. His concerto for two trumpets, is now established as one of the major works for the trumpet.

WAGNER, Richard (1813-83) German composer who wrote his first opera at the age of 19. His famous opera in which he produced a new kind of music-drama that combined music, word, action and decor was "The Ring of the Nibelungs."

PERFORMERS

VIOLIN

The tradition of the violin virtuoso who dazzles with his or her technical brilliance is no less alive than it was a hundred years ago.

Yehudi Menuhin

The violin is also being used again, as it was originally, as a popular instrument. Outstanding players include Kyung-Wha Chung, Nigel Kennedy, Stephane Grapelli, Yehudi Menuhin, Nathan Milstein, David Oistrakh, and Itzhak Perlman. Jascha Heifetz (1901-87) was a Lithuanian-born violinist. He was known for the technical expertise of his performances, and for the speed at which he played some pieces!

FLUTE

In medieval times the recorder was the most widely played solo woodwind instrument. Music began to be written for the flute in the 17th century, and it has been an instrument popular with composers ever since. Vivaldi, Handel, Bach, and Mozart, all wrote sonatas for solo flute. Today, the flute and other woodwind instruments are used in jazz, folk, and rock, as well as in classical music. Outstanding flute players of our day include Jean-Pierre Rampal from France, Paul Edmund Davies, William Bennett, Susan Milan from Britain, Julius Baker, Paul Meisen from Germany, and Peter-Lukas Graf from Switzerland.

Paul Edmund

TRUMPET

Over the past 300 years there have been many great virtuoso performers of the trumpet. The 18th century included performers, such as

Chet Baker

Johann Ernst Altenburg, who was also a composer, and Anton Weidinger, a Vietnamese trumpeter who gave some of the first performances of Haydn's trumpet concerto. Outstanding players of this century include Bix Biederbecke, Maurice Andre, Adolph Herseth, Miles Davis, and John Faddis. Jazz trumpeters include Louis Armstrong, Chet Baker and more recently, Hugh Masekela.

KEYBOARDS

By the modern period (from 1900) grand pianos had a beautiful sound which composer-pianists, such as Debussy and Ravel, were greatly inspired by. Later, American pianist and songwriter, George Gershwin (1898-1937) was inspired by the rhythms and harmonies of the new dance music, jazz. His famous "Rhapsody in Blue" is a kind of jazz concerto for piano and orchestra. Black pianist, Scott Joplin (1868-1917) is remembered for his piano pieces called "rags." Other jazz pianists include Art Tatum, Thomas "Fats" Waller. Austrian performer, Alfred Brendel is a famous classical pianist.

Alfred Brendel

Glossary

accidental: on a sheet of written music, a sharp, flat or natural that is not shown in the key signature

arco: playing with the bow, as distinct from *pizzicato* (see below)

bar: time unit into which a piece of music is divided, corresponding to the meter (which is usually regular) of the piece

blues: a basic jazz style, often a song

boogie: speeded-up blues, often for the piano

chamber music: music for small groups of players, once designed to be played in private homes

cantata: a word used to describe almost every sort of work for voice (or voices) with instrumental accompaniment

chord: any combination of notes that is played or sung at the same time

classical: a word sometimes used to describe "highbrow" music; musicians use it to define only the period from Bach to Beethoven

clef: on a sheet of written music, the sign at the beginning of a line, indicating the pitch of the lines and spaces of the stave

concerto: a composition for solo instrument and orchestra

crotchet: on a sheet of written music, the basic time unit of Western music

dotted note: indicates that the time value of the note is increased by half

dynamics: commands telling you how loud or soft to play

embouchure: shaping the lips to the mouthpiece of a wind instrument

flat: note lowered in pitch by a half step

frequency: the scientific measurement of pitch

harmonics or harmonic: a series of notes that can be played using the same valve or valves, or as open notes, without using any valves at all

key: incidates the major or minor scale in which music is written; also, one of the levers on the piano which causes a note to sound

key signature: on a sheet of written music, the group of sharps or flats at the beginning of each line showing which notes are to be "sharpened" or "flattened" throughout the section following

improvisation: when the players make up the music as they go along. Jazz is mostly improvisation

interval: the distance in pitch between two notes. The interval between the strings on the violin, is called a perfect fifth

ledger line: line added to the musical staff for notes too high or low to fit within the staff

GLOSSARY

metronome: machine that sounds regular beats at a speed that can be adjusted. The figures on the metronome indicate the number of beats per minute

mute: any device which, by being attached to an instrument, damps down or subdues its normal tone

natural: on a sheet of written music, indicates the cancellation of a sharp or flat which would otherwise be expected

octave: the interval between eight natural notes. The notes making up an octave interval have the same letter name, and similar characteristics so that we hear them as virtually the "same" note

oratorio: any large-scale concert work based on a religious subject, written for soloists, chorus and orchestra

piston valve: a device that allows the air column inside a trumpet to pass straight through the valve, but which, when pressed down diverts the air along a length of tubing called a valve slide.

pitch: the highness or lowness of a note

pizzicato: plucking

quaver: a time unit having half the value of a crotchet

rest: a silent beat in a piece of music

rock and roll: a dance style based on boogie-woogie

rotary valve: a device that allows the air column to pass straight through the valve, but is also able to divert the air by 45 degrees when rotated in its casing

scale: the sequence of neighboring notes on which music is based. Western scales are generally made up of steps of a tone or a semitone

semitone: the smallest interval of the conventional Western scale

sharp: on a sheet of paper, indicates that the pitch of a note is to be raised by a semi-tone

sonata: a composition, often for solo piano

staff: (or stave) on a sheet of written music, the lines on which notes of the same pitch are played as one (five in modern western music)

technique: the mechanical aspect of playing an instrument, and basis for advanced music playing

tie: a line indicating that two notes of the same pitch are played as one

tutti: the whole orchestra playing together, without the soloist

virtuoso: an outstandingly skilled player or singer who overcomes the greatest difficulties in music with apparent ease

INDEX

INDEX

INDEX

Photo Credits